Communions With Christ

*Mystical Revelations
Of Infinite Wisdom
From Our Creator*

by

Sharon Ellis

Copyright © 2008 by SHARON ELLIS

COMMUNIONS WITH CHRIST
by Sharon Ellis

Printed in the United States of America

ISBN 978-1-60647-889-9

Communions With Christ is the sole and exclusive property of author Sharon Ellis.

All rights reserved solely by the author and her assigned heirs. The author guarantees all contents are original and do not infringe upon the legal rights of any other person or work. No part of this book may be reproduced or utilized in any way or form, or by any means, without the express permission of the author. The views expressed in this book are not necessarily those of the publisher.

Unless otherwise indicated, Bible quotations are taken from the Life Application Study Bible, New International Version of the Bible. Copyright © 1988 by Tyndale House Publishers, Inc. and Zondervan Publishing House.

www.xulonpress.com

To place a book order call toll-free 1-866-909-BOOK (2665), or e-mail: bookorder@xulonpress.com

You may notice that any reference to satan will not be capitalized. This is by grammatical choice because God specifically told the author that satan is very small and never to be capitalized.

Communions With Christ, **by Sharon Ellis,** is available to full time bookstores and retailers through Distributors:
Ingram Book Company,
order toll free 1-800-937-8000
and
Spring Arbor Distributors, Inc.
Order toll free 1-800-395-4340

Communions With Christ, **by Sharon Ellis,** can be ordered through your local book store or from the following book stores and e-retailers:
Amazon.com; Barnes & Noble; Borders; Target

Communions With Christ

FOREWORD

From: Dr. M.V. Myre, Ph.D. June 12, 2006

When Sharon first asked me to read her writings, I didn't know what to expect. I knew that she was a deeply faithful Christian. I knew she wrote well, having seen some anecdotes and devotions that she had written. **I didn't know that when she said she had heard the voice of Jesus that she meant quite literally!**

Sharon wanted me to read what she had written to get my opinion as Pastor and as "Old Testament Scholar". (I have a Ph.D. in Hebrew Bible from Southern Methodist University). But my response to her writing had more to do with the interior life of faith and the heart knowledge of the seeker rather than with the head knowledge of the academic.

These writings remind me almost at once of the Christian mystics that I read in seminary: that sense of closeness with God, that sense of joy in Christ's presence, that sense of personal word being given, that sense of obedience to writing down what is given even if not fully understood. These writings have made me think and made me laugh. They sometimes confuse me, but in the end they inspire me to more fully grasp the heart of the Savior.

I told Sharon that not everyone would understand these writings, but that they should be shared. Does Jesus really speak to us like this in this day and time? Does Jesus really love us and laugh with us as these writings suggest? You decide. But, I hope when you read them, you will also be drawn into the presence of the Holy and Gracious One who seeks to communicate with us in so many ways every day. I hope that you will take the opportunity to listen for the voice of Jesus in your own life and will have the courage to believe what you hear.

[Dr. M. V. Myre is a respected Pastor and theologian possessing a vast Biblical knowledge who received a Ph.D. in Religious Studies at Southern Methodist University and who also taught Christian classes at Perkins School of Theology.]

Communions With Christ

THIS IS A TRUE STORY

"What I like about this book
is that I know
it all really happened.
because I was there."

John Ellis

I've witnessed what I would call a bending in time.
I've seen Sharon's spirit being lifted into God's realm
and then brought back again.
I've seen her spirit be engulfed by God
and then released to do his work.

I've seen her constant faithfulness to God's plan.
Without this miracle of God's help
I know she would not have been able to do it on her own.
God seems to always use the unequipped
and equip them with what they need.
He has done so with my wife, Sharon.
Her fallow fields have been planted by God
and miraculous gifts of bounty have sprung forth.
He has dressed her in His armor
and sent her to battle and He has been victorious.
&
It's not over yet!
That's how I see it as Sharon's husband, John.

Communions With Christ

DEDICATION

As dear as this tribute is,
I can only come up to the mark by yielding
to God and say,
this is entirely His,
so,
thank You, Christ.
Amen.

Sharon Ellis

~~~~~~~~~~

This is a True Story

Communions With Christ

CONTENTS

I WENT UP 15

MY BACKGROUND 19

THE ANGEL 23

THE ANGEL'S COMMUNICATION 27

GOD'S ANGEL, ARCHANGEL 35

LIVE OAK 39

WORDS AND NUMBERS 43

CORPUS CHRISTI 47

THE ANGEL'S SONG 53

SHERMAN 59

WHITE FALCONER 63

KNOWINGS – GOD'S GIFTS 69

QUESTIONS 73

SEEDS 79

DAVID AND JOB	83
GOD'S SAVING GRACE	89
WISDOM OF CHILDREN	97
MELODEE	99
SHARON	103
SONG	107
GOD'S REVELATIONS	109
INDEPENDENCE	111
I CANCEL OUT THE PLACE	113
PENCILS	115
THE ERASER	119
LUNCH TIME	125
CHOIR PRACTICE	127
SING ALONG	131
PLOWING FIELDS	137
GEE	139
TELL ME	143
BAPTISM	153
CLIMB UP	157

THE BOAT 163

ELIJAH 169

WHO ME? 173

BUOY 177

I LET YOU 179

WOMAN JETS AND EMERGE
GAMMA RAYS 181

HOLOGRAPHIC EXISTENCE, THE
WINDOW TO PASS INTO THE ONE 185

SEVEN SEALS 191

HOLY UNTO YOU 193

PLEASE UNDERSTAND 199

I SAW MY PRIESTHOOD
GIVEN UNTO ME 205

REASONABLE CONCLUSION 211

Communions With Christ

I WENT UP

Written on June 8, 2006

I went up. That is what it seems. The place of Himself. Just up.

Even saying 'up' I know I do not mean literally. For 'up' is a mere direction of man's vocabulary. And so I must try, oh try, oh how I try, to state the spiritual out of the corporeal language.

I went above. Or, I mean higher. Gosh, the word does not exist.

I went through a great divide. This divide takes the seeker nearer to Whom is sought. I went across the planes and mountains of the great divide, which of course did not have any plane* or mountain as earth knows the definition. Only, I seek to say that some of my days as a human being in the pursuit of Favor seemed at once serene as well as tumultuous. Feelings of tumultuous reverie accompanied with favor as a pool of glass.

This pool of glass was Himself in glad tidings sent. Yellow was the surface of the glass, not gold, or white, but yellow. And I know not yet what that color means to the whole perspective, yet I was given the pool of glass. Stable. Transparent. Level. All Telling. Ever sending me the reflections of King Jesus — the Throne Room's place — the temple Tales. What will be and is to come. A look. A privilege. A tone. A song.

In the crossing of this great divide, Jesus made, without any doubt, my heart into a man of faith.

Three things I wish to make clear to the reader of my attempts to convey spiritual ecstasy.

One: all of these mysteries are none of my creation. They come not from a mind set on earthly things but from a mind trained to see.

The second point is that, as might be obvious, the Trainer of my seeing is Christ. All Holy Spirit's Joy. Father God's Excellent Grace. Favor. And my sheer delight to say, God Himself.

I do not, nor did not, nor will not initiate any of what I recount to you as other than from God Himself, as, having taken the path beyond, at great sacrifice and full pain, and by the hand of my Lord's Will, He Himself sat at lecture time, and study time, and book time, and secret open spiritual meetings time — all the time. And He my Sovereign did oh so faithfully teach me His Voice - above the trains of thought of man - above wanderings of my own mind - outside of all that I am as mortal.

God absolutely taught me His Voice.

And so, as my life depends upon a recounting that will not offend my King of Truth Himself, I walk in held high head of knowing that the words I say come from Jesus are those of Him. Pure. And, as peculiar as some seem, yet as such, are simply part of the talk He shares and requests me to write down and share.

Many the days and nights I have pondered His messages. At times a new revelation will spring out of this at some later month or year — apparently then I am ready.

Finally, the third point I want to state is that — as Jesus prayed for His apostles to become one with the Father and with Him — He said: *"Not for them alone do I pray but for all who believe in me."* and again: *"I am in them."*

Therefore I must say that the Father has granted His only Son's prayer and made me one inside of Himself ~ and in such a mystery is truly showing me with higher eyes all that, as Love, is higher.

Where we come again to that word 'higher'.
I am in the middle of this journey, having crossed to the other side, yet now seeing all that I was taken here to see. Higher is the place I live, within His work, that I have agreed to do in just Mercy sent to me. Higher is my calling than I could have ever dreamed from my horrid beginnings, yet all the more Glory does God receive for proving to me, a simple soul, that He is beyond description in His divine redemption and just Goodness to a mere single soul of near death in the world.

Holy is His name. And so, I continue to walk, and talk with God, because He continues to walk and talk with me. His gifts are exquisite, and far more splendid than those of earth. His fathering is kindness.
Kindness Father's me.
His Glory should shine out of all that I write about Him, but if I fail, just know that I do love my Lord Jesus.

~~~~~~~~~~

| * plane: 1. Mathematics. A surface containing all the straight lines that connect any two points on it. 2. A flat or level surface. 3. A level of development, existence, or achievement. |

Communions With Christ

MY BACKGROUND

The fact is, I was a Biblical Illiterate.
I was unschooled in the ways of the Christian faith.
I very clearly was as totally a blank and un-sullied* plate as God could have chosen to come and write His Heartfelt Word upon.

My parents did not teach me anything about God, for their ways were to fight and scream the name of God in vain as fountains of wrath spewed constantly upon me during my growing up years.

I speak as kindly as I can of those days, the days of my youthful ignorance from God, yet it is relevant to know that I was a totally hollow and unfilled vessel which was ready to be dropped in on mightily by His Highness — for I was literally death bound and extremely ill in my prison of anxieties, fears, phobias, and uncontrollable fear of people or any social situation. I hid from life, and I died in my youth. I was doing my best to ambulate about the earth, for the sake of my two sons and husband, but the truth is, I was dead and fast asleep, and thusly, driven by anger, hatred, unforgiveness, and all the things that result through massive abuses to a child from the people you would hope would be different.

My husband John did a good job of following his upbringing of being an alter boy and going to Catholic school and his masses. The truth is, he was totally burned out on (what the future man I would marry) called the hypocrisy that resided in the walls of the church he attended, and so, he dropped his heart out of the quest for God. At least he had been in a quest, and during this time, he did learn some basic things about the faith.

On the other hand, from all perspectives, I was dormant, unplanted, under the soil of nothing growing here, and factually dead to this world, dead to any world. Depressed.

Under the circumstances of never attending church while growing up, it takes a miracle to transform and resurrect the mind that the world has killed and buried **in fears.**

For the record, our God is a Miracle Making God, and He will do a miracle if a heart that is dead is calling out to be alive, ... Oh please, Jesus help me to be alive, if there is anything at all to what people say that you are!

It is there that I found myself one evening.

Darkness of mind, and on my knees, saying to someone that people call 'Jesus' ... "Jesus, I am dead and buried in my tomb. Please let me live before I die, if you are really the Lord they say you are, help me. I cannot go any lower into my tomb of death. ... Well ... thanks."

I was almost 40 years old with two teenaged sons and a fairly complacent husband who died a long time ago too, in his soul I mean.

~~~~~~~~~~

[sully: 1. To mar the cleanliness or luster of soil or stain. 2. To defile, taint.]

God used the word 'un-sullied' to write His dissertation, and so, when I looked the word up, 'sully', and found 'sully' to mean ' to mar the cleanness of soil or stain', my goodness what the Holy Spirit told me! I was 'soil', and also 'stain', because I am 'inked' into the photo graph that His Holiness God draws up over the years of life. It will become evident to the reader that my soil or stain was undisturbed by religion as I and God had never met before this encounter.

Another revelation came to me. God described me as "soil", as in the Bible there are soils mentioned. Scriptures explain what kind of soil takes the seeds and grows to become fit for the Kingdom.

In my case I was "un-sullied" soil, very importantly, in that I was ignorant of any religion's direction. There was not any 'religion' in me to mar the stain which God would use to mold me, or to disrupt the soil that God intended to plant in. I was a soil undisturbed by the religions of the world or the way that humans interpret their slants. God took me, soil unsullied, and He wielded His plow and furrowed my years, and He said the words into me that grew my holy time into a planted seed of fruitfulness that is good to taste.

God is amazing. Amen.

Communions With Christ

THE ANGEL

Year: 1987

I was in the middle of the incredible miracle from God when I saw the angel Raphael.

Majesty from Joy. Intelligent communication from a being from nowhere I had ever experienced. Intellectual Joy was to be mine, for a moment, as well as ecstasy.

I was clutching the hand of my husband John after a seemingly endless mental analytical preparation to get myself to walk across the atrium inside of a mall. My heart rate was rapid. Fear overtaking me. Surely I could get to the other side of the large open space without dying. Past the strangers. Past the escalator. Into the artery that led to the movie theatre.

John wanted to go see some movie. I was trying to accompany him in spite of my massive state of fright at just about everything that was.

Agoraphobia mushroomed. Giant waves of fear heaving up and down within me. Step. Step, step. My feet were lead weights.

My thoughts were so turned inward that I was a morbid self centered mess, mulling over the exact plan in my head. I would sit on the end seat, of the last row of the theatre, and I would go pee pee first before being trapped behind closed doors when, of course, my claustrophobia would add itself to my list of plights. I would not drink any liquid so I wouldn't have an accident, and I would cover my eyes in the bad parts of the movie that might frighten me, and I would stick my fingers in my ears and hide my head in my lap with my arms covering my head in case of incoming mortars if there was screaming or violent intentions portrayed by the actors in the movie. As soon as the movie started I would begin counting down the seconds to the end of my agony which I had pre-determined would be one hour and 58 minutes of movie running time, and I would try to need nothing of John. I would try to make myself as invisible as possible so that no one could see me being panic stricken. And I would tell myself that the hot flush which would come up was not going to kill me today. I would be physically present but in my inner state of Terror. And I would repeat over and over in my head 'Just a little longer and you are safe'.

Step. Step, step.
The movie ticket window was still about seventy five yards away.
I hardly was able to think about anything but doom.

Then — my world changed, by the hand of God.

Suddenly I sensed something hovering above my head. Fear made me react quickly. I instinctively looked up while lowering my body in a defensive bracing for a physical blow which was my post traumatic stress syndrome thinking — from being hit in the head unexpectedly while growing up.

I saw an angel.

The hair stood straight up on my arms in an electrical sensory response and from an electrical being interacting with my heart-strings, and it was divine and unexplainable.

A mighty ... holy ... angel.
Blue ... sapphire ... peace.

I saw hope.
Love sent rays of hope in the shape of an angel of goodness.

The massive atrium was covered by a huge dome of glass towering three stories high. Out of this open sky, out of these open heavenly splendid filters, a being generated from miraculous origins.

Angels appear to people they intend to impart messages to. My angel had a walloping message for me, but I was not prepared for it at all.

A feeling came over me that gave me goose bumps.

I felt the peace of God drop into my heart, and no fear existed for the moments that the angel spoke to me.

I am sent to you, Sharon. Fear not.

He sang. The angel sang. A song so beautiful that my heart wept and my soul was transformed forever.

A music of sorts, no, a voice, and yet, yes, music.

I heard within me a pitch. It was flowing. Flowing along on a charted course. Coursing along on a chorded thread. Kinetically withstanding the flow. Immersing the tune in holy waters.

Love ... Light. Song. Joy. Beauty. It was connected to something that was the source of its emanation. I was hearing the angel speak to me within myself!

I am Healer. I am Raphael. I am an angel of David's Lord. I come in the name of the Healer.

It was superb to be in the middle of such a peaceful understanding of an angelic communication, even though I had no idea as to its higher meaning.

Generously allowing me into the awareness of him the angel took my mind and spirit into another realm, a place where there is peace and faith and love, and wonders untold to man.

Communions With Christ

THE ANGEL'S COMMUNICATION

I could see an angel!

I do not proclaim to understand the order or reasoning behind God's will. I am only recording it as it happened.

In a single life altering glimpse it registered on me that I was seeing an angel and that he had something to tell me. The angel was taking me into a higher level of awareness than I ever knew existed.

Soaring into his spiritual wisdom and flow, gathering earthly dimensional properties to radiate to me as a creature whom I saw in my perspective, the angel moved around as a free and singular entity.

The veil of angelic dominions is very rarely taken up to this level of interferon radiation levels, and so we rarely seem to be in your realms, but today it will be so, in order that I may tell you something.

I had no idea what the angel meant by 'taken up to this level of interferon radiation levels', but it was so lovely that I just registered the words as wonderful. They went to my very DNA and sat there, waiting, growing. Throughout this experience I was always growing in my understanding of the human words to put to the holy sounds.

The angel's presence took me up. Into heavenly places where language is so different. The sounds were angelic and in keys that were other world to my dictionary or word base.

For this moment the angel just made me know what the earth could not tell me, ever.

Holy yardsticks measure the tunes and your resonance pitches the resonance off of walls. These walls reside in the earth's atmosphere, and so, interferon levels must traject to be the angelic appearance I am.

I understood for that moment that the angel was explaining God's creative properties and trying to find human words. I knew the angel had freight to carry, or a sort of composition of himself, and that the freight of this composition had to alter for my eyes to see this apparition. I was mesmerized to say the least. The angel explained the metric system of height and told me he was twelve in human terms. If this meant twelve feet tall, I am not fortunate enough to have retained that bit of truth, because the only thing I remember the angel explaining God doing was making him twelve, and this was a measure of sorts. God's height is not ours and our terms are not the heavenly ones. I knew this, and it mattered to me that I would not take away the full understanding. I searched the vision and knew this was outside of myself, not interior, but truly exterior in perspective to myself.

I also knew relatively speaking that the angel was not near nor far but that he was just the angel.

I absolutely knew that the angelic transformation that I was witnessing take place (within the realms of earth's space and time) formed itself by a will of iron, a place unmovable, a force unchangeable, a pitch above any octave known to mans' ears; and it pealed, projected, and transmitted into my being a perfect understanding of the fact that peace exists above any level I will hope to know as mortal man.

I am sent to you, Sharon. Fear not. I am Healer. I am Raphael. I am an angel of David's Lord. I come in the name of the Healer.

Sweetness has the ability to take away the cares of the world, while surrounded by sweetness.

By the way, Raphael, (I spoke inside myself), why do you rotate within juxtaposed lines that overlay themselves? And ... are you making me know these obvious scientific things?

I had no idea why I even thought that question, except that the angel must, to please me, have given me the answer that was a question which I did not know how to formulate. I had never used the word 'juxtaposed' in my life and had no idea what it meant. When I said it, suddenly I saw that the angel had a sort of other plane of existence, and he, that is the angelic dominion of himself, took shape inside of this world, along side the other world, and it, the lines juxtaposed overlaying the planes, were him, the angel, in triplicate and more than triplicate, they undeniably just took infinity and traveled with this region beyond my registry, but the sight (that was a clue) sort of came to me, so that I could register his presence to my normal eyesight.

Angel, (I spoke inside myself again), humbly I report that I don't understand. I practically failed all my math and science classes in high school. So therefore I refused to take any math or science in college ... so angel ... sir ... I mean, Raphael ... I don't know what this all means ... oh, you know that already ...

Very simple really. The Maker that takes all things into account takes my sighted purpose and elevates the radial compass that is His to manipulate and allows the level your eyes see to focus their trajectory unto my inner purpose, and these days will be jolly, these days you will have coming unto you.

For the record, I did not get this understanding until several years later, years of training in the Lord's ways, and by God Himself. I was, however, imprinted with the unearthly sciences of angelic transmissions, and then, in God's own time, allowed to have the words to explain these things.

It took a long time to process, afterwards, (years really), that what I may take away from these words, these keys of music, was a form of true communication from angelic realms. I did not understand it then.

At that time, Raphael was so dear that I just registered it all.

For some reason it imprinted as fact, a sweet angelic fact, that gave me recall later when I tried to write down my experience. I think I was given an indelible memory that I could recall, but the fact is, I was not given the understanding. Not then. I was just taken up, and spoken to.

Interferon levels of radiation simply refers to the junk that thermally globs about in the earth, and makes the place a solar burner. In this place, as an angel, it is taken from you by the angelic thermal registry that hauls garbage out of the person assigned to the angel. As the Nurturer of the friend we are given in earth ~ an angel has the responsibility to transfer all levels of interferon out of the planetary zones and to rectify all calculations to adjust the mankind's elements into transferable trajectory which will enable you to be sent above the planet's third dimensional sound barrier reef and soar towards the Fourth Seal.

Apparently my mind must have registered some sort of question about what the "fourth seal" was because I suddenly was aware of this answer from the angel.

It is the barrier through which is the entry to heaven, so sealed is the Fourth Seal.

I got a picture inside of my heart of a great wall, divided by dimensions, and the Maker of these was God.

Just listen, Sharon. Hear the entry opening. Just listen, Sharon ...

Great that thou art oh woman of great perfume, and great thou art oh woman of justice, and listen thou will, to the Maker's tunes!

It was amazing, the simplest thing occurred to me. I was lost! It seemed so silly to be lost — to have a sense of being lost, to be not found or rooted in a sense of being found whole, because here with this angel I felt the entire place of safety and foundness and I wanted it.

Laughter is healing. Fun is my balm to you. Holy fun. Prepare for the joy ride towards healing. Inside the Fourth Seal all Majesty travels towards fullness, and above is Five and Six and Seven. Seals.

I was suddenly aware that the angel lived outside of the restrictions of any sort of time. Or maybe I realized that there is all time existing at once where angles live. It all happened so fast that I was hardly able to grasp it before I was given higher still.

Without any difficulty at all I realized that his domain is actually degrees of rotating light, sent by way of a vector transference, by wonders man has yet to comprehend.

Pealing their waltz at me, these degrees of rotating light suspended into my realm the shape and contour of an angel.

It was really all quite simple.

I was seeing the properties of light, and within these are the properties of love, and within these are God's creative radius taking form — as ever it does within the third dimension of our earth.

Put on this habit, woman. Put on this holy habit.

Raphael held out towards me what looked like a long brown monk's robe, or a priest's robe, with a hood on it. It looked to me like a garment which would be worn by a holy person who had decided to cloister himself up on a mountain top to devote his life to communing with God.

The priestly robe was transferred into my hand which was stretched out towards the suspended life that handed it to me.

"Okay." I agreed.

Simply put, I knew that I was willing to do what ever the angel Raphael had come to tell me was going to happen.

My Maker allows my emanation to you, Sharon, so that I may help you realize your calling.

"My calling?"

God calls you, blessed Sharon.

I realized that there is a God.

The angel was veiling his assignment, though I did not know it, for my shock rate was unable, or unready, to take the full message at what was this moment in my life.

Time seemed to be suspended. Time was no longer any sort of element within the presence of the angel's appearance to me.
Surrounding this angel, above him and behind him, I could see the towering glass atrium rotunda that John and I stood beneath. As the sun light passed through the glass the angel took shape and penetrated my awareness with his being. He was a beautiful image of what appeared to be pieces of white light come together to form a delicate lace image.
The head of the angel was obscured by a great white light — penetrating with radiance and beauty — in a halo formation, making it impossible for me to see his face.
Suspended within his divine mission, he told me things in notes, sounds floating into my being, my heart, the place where life is, and evermore desires to hear these notes play eternally with grace.
Moving here and there, gathering radiance and beauty, energy from heaven came down and spoke to my heart. A ... overture. I heard the whistling of winds passing by the door that opened from heaven, and divine talk formed within this place I was in.

A great healing is coming upon you, woman.

Raphael's voice was a key, a melody that I heard as a note, musical in tone, playing in a frequency that was resonant within me. Joyfully I knew that this vision and angelic appearance was meant to convey some sort of wisdom or interpretation to me, God only knows what, for at the time that this happened to me my inner person was a devoid and barren wasteland of nothing spiritual whatsoever to connect the dots for any Godly wisdom then.

I trembled and shook with the sudden realization of the greatness that had appeared to me. I watched Raphael as he took leave of me, but the kindly Person who sent this angel to me allowed the angel to tell me one more thing before the angel left my comprehension.

The Healer who sent me shall send me to you again, Sharon.

Then, the angel disappeared.

~~~~~~~~~

Psalm 8: 9 *"Oh LORD, our Lord, how majestic is your name in all the earth!"*

Now in this earth there is a Power that warns and builds, tells and fills up, this Power takes the people of earth who invite Him into their lives and fixes them, if allowed to do so, and He does it His way.

GOD'S ANGEL, ARCHANGEL

"**D**o you see that, John?" My knees were buckling and my feet took root in the spot, never wanting to leave.

My hand slipped out of John's hand as he continued walking towards the movie theatre. Had all of this happened so quickly?

"John!" I called loudly, yet, I think I was whispering, faint as the times had made my body.

"Come on. We're gunna be late." John glanced back at the ever growing distance between us, since that magnificent encounter had made my legs crumble and unable to move.

"I can't go to a movie now!" I snapped with the annoying realization that I was back in planet earth with ignorance as my dwelling companion. "I just saw an angel!"

"An angel?" At least John stopped walking and turned to come back to me.

"What does 'David's Lord' mean? Who is Raphael?"

"Let's go. The movie is starting."

"Can you see anything?" I looked longingly back into the place where my spirit took me, but the place had vanished from my habitually restricted earth bound flesh.

"No." John looked up at the very spot where the angel had appeared.

"He said I was going to be a priest."

"Who?"

"The angel! Aren't you paying attention?"

"You can't be a priest! You're married and you're a women. I don't think an angel would tell you you're gunna be a priest. That's really offensive to me."

"The angel said his name is Raphael. Did you ever hear the name Raphael for an angel?

"You're kidding, right?

"You were an alter boy! Help me, John!" I was getting grossly impatient towards the fleshly tendency to waste time getting to the obviously necessary things.

"Raphael is an Archangel."

"What's an ark angel?

"Are you for real? I know you never went to church but you've gotta be kidding. You know what an Archangel is, right?"

"No."

John just stared at me. He stared at the entry to the movie theatre. I could see it in his eyes that he sort of gave up his intentions to ever see his afternoon movie.

"An Archangel is one of the really big angels. Higher in rank or something." John was looking at my reactions closely. Deciding if he had any ability to believe what he was hearing from me.

"If I had a message from an ark angel would it be important?"

"What message?

"I heard him say he is an angel of David's Lord, and his name is Raphael, and he comes in the name of the healer, and I will become a priest, and he gave me a monk's robe or a priest's rode, and he said put on this holy habit woman, and he said God is calling me, and he said he will come back to talk to me again, and also some scientific stuff that I need to think about to remember."

"I think we should still go to the movie."

"I can't believe you, John! Go ahead then but I'm finding a bookstore!"

My tracks made hast to the nearest bookstore in the mall, fear and anxiety pushed way back on the back burner to my happy desire to find out the angel's name's meaning and what the meaning of it all could be.

Right now! I want the answer today! Now! And no messing around!

So, I took a long time searching. An hour at least! Asking clerks with no results, flipping through books. Bookstores should have answers, right? But, nothing.

John was leaning at the entryway, waiting as I came out. I was dejected.

"Maybe you're looking in the wrong place. That's not a Christian bookstore."

"Of course! Oh thank you, John!" I hugged my husband. Ran to a kiosk and found a phone book. Bookstores. Bookstores, Christian. "John, there's none in the mall! We have to go drive to one! Hurry before they close!"

Cokesbury Christian Bookstore. I flew out of the car and undressed the contents of several books — spewing trails of anger and frustration behind me. Exasperated with my lack of connection to anything relevant. Solemn. Defeated. I hung my head and stopped looking. I started to cry with my hands pressed at the railing of a large square book display.

"Here." John held two books in his hands. "The Catholic Bible and this book."

I looked up at his face. He simply provided me the answer, so easily, no striving, just the answer for my seeker's heart.

There it was. In print. The words I needed to see. Next to a beautiful Byzantine painting of the Arch Angel Raphael. *"Raphael, Archangel of the Lord. Meaning of the name Raphael: Healer."*

Slowly, somewhat more reverently, I took the Catholic Bible in my hands and began to read from the Book of Tobit the encounters of the Angel Raphael who came and provided healing, even though the people whom he helped did not know who he really was. And so, I knew. Within all of me that life is, inside me, I knew. And no man on this earth could from this point on forever until the eternal life that lies beyond ever convince me that I did not encounter the angel Raphael. For he himself had introduced himself to me and said, *"I am Healer. I am Raphael. I am an angel of David's Lord. I come in the name of the Healer."*

Now. If I could just figure out who David's Lord was? And how I could become a priest when I was married and I had two teenaged sons?

What the beginning did not tell me was that there would be no end. I would always have another question, and each answer that I was to be given would give me so many more questions!

Possibly that would be a part of the healing, the making my mind so fervent for the answers that I sought to be outside of my small dead world and began to give myself leave to go have a life after all.

~~~~~~~~~

Communions With Christ

LIVE OAK
Quercus Virginiana

Year: 1988

Live Oak. I had a Live Oak tree in my front yard. John and our two sons had built me a front deck of wood to sit on and an Adirondack style wooden chair to sit in.

I loved to come outside to sit under the oak, just to think, being the mental analytical person that I am. For years I had watched the blue jays build their nests and have babies, and the brilliant red cardinals come to perch in the branches of the stately oak as it grew larger and larger and rooted deeper and deeper. Of course the mockingbirds were there, too.

So much wild life. Squirrels and lizards. Monarch butterflies and hummingbirds. And baby oaks, too, each year sprouting up from acorns all around the original oak. I gardened here. I placed my creative hand print upon the space. It all allowed me time to meditate on the things going on in my life.

For the life of me I could not now figure out why these things were happening, but these things were happening. Supernatural things.

On this particular morning holy reverie had taken me over. As I watched through the spaces of the live oak branches the light that came in gave me remembrance of the angel's swirling light particles. Rays of filtered splendor.

I heard a meeooww.

Peace. I was at peace.
I heard a tiny meow. A cat.
A kitten, crying out, "Come get me!"
Peace under my Live Oak tree.

The tiny flecks of light translated to me wisdom by the swaying boughs of my Giant Oak. I heard a cat crying. Calling me. It was a voice I wanted to take to my heart, the heart that it was ... I wanted this heart, too — a Voice I understood from somewhere that God had made for me.

I stood up. Searched. I looked high and low about my yard and finally found this tiny cat, a young great golden kitten, sitting high on a limb of my old stately oak.

Meeoow. A third time.

I heard my Master's Voice.
Peace.

Come here little cat. Oh you beautiful lion! You are a jolly nice lion.
Great divine destiny at work.
I plucked down the kitten from the oak. He had long soft fur and a magnificent face.
What are you doing up there?
The cat began to purrrr. He was only a few weeks old.
Where did you come from?

Judah.

God spoke to me, but I did not know what this rich gift was, not then.
I like that name! I'll call you Judah! Are you mine?
God sent me this cat. God told me his name. Judah.

Allow Judah's love to grow in your heart, Sharon. I love you, Sharon.

I took this kitten for my own. I named him Judah. I fed him and allowed him to live in my home. To hear him purr, hear his voice, hear his heart. To hear the bell of Judah's life gave me joy and brought health to my hurting world.

Judah. My lion in a tiny golden cat.

I was very lonely ... wounded so deeply inside. I was a gnarled and fruitless garden that grew nothing but tragedy. I made up my own tragedy because I did not trust anyone. I did not believe anyone loved me. I was still the imprinted message of my youth. I still heard the shouting of my father's hatred and his anger telling me how unlovable I was and that he wished I was never born.

Jesus does amazing things and we don't really even know what the thing is that is healing us until the time goes by and we look back and see the progress along the way. I think it would be nice to give praise to the Healer who healeth we.

Some weeks later, while I was sitting once again under the limbs of the Live Oak, thinking things over, I had a vision. Whereas I now thought I was lost and completely unusable, I would one day understand the things coming into my future and God would talk to me and He would ask of me, "Are you the man who comes from Judah?" And I would say, "I am."

I could see my future. I could see myself sitting under another oak, in another place, at a future time, and this future moment would be explaining to me something that was meant for my journey to know. I saw in my vision that God was talking to me, and He would be telling me something about Judah ~ and I would understand and I would cry from the depths of me with the revelation of understanding.

I did not know how this could possibly take place.

~~~~~~~~~~

Communions With Christ

WORDS AND NUMBERS

Year: 1988 Onward ...

Words and numbers. They would come into my head at the most amazing times.

I was worried all the time. That is a part of growing up with torment. One worries about the imprinting great torment that surely will befall a victim of great torment. I knew no other way of thinking, or really of living, except to be worried and in a state of simple anxiety all the time.

So, along with the analyst brain that I was given in life, were the results of my childhood domestic violence. I worried almost all the time about the most inconsequential of details up to the most tremendously important of life's issues.

The anxiety had worn my stamina down and taken my life away from me.

I was greatly impaired.

In life, one has to interact to get along well.

I was not sure how to accomplish that social interaction and so I remained, by choice, alone. My fears were to the degree that I could not even go out of my front door to check our daily mail delivery, because that required me to walk past our front deck, down the street past three strangers' houses, to the community mailbox, all by myself! Oh TERROR! Your own imagination can only subtract from the terrible things I managed to think up. Life in the mind of FEAR transcends sanity or rational thinking.

I only ventured out of the house with a 'safe person' with me. After all, one never knew the unexpected hour that any given explosion could erupt, did one? Bombs came exploding unexpectedly. I well knew from years of unexpected grenades being thrown at me while I grew up, leaving me a mangled mental cripple boxed into an ever shrinking world inside of an impenetrable shell of fear.

I did not trust anything or anyone.

I sort of gave myself license to believe that I was not crazy.

I sort of knew that seeing an angel and my strange new experiences came from Love. I felt this as Truth. I knew this as Certain.

Something Good was happening to me!

The angel's appearance had caused me to start going out alone, farther and farther, until I finally drove to the neighboring community library alone, without my safe person. These trips out of my house were a phenomenal achievement. To me, they were like climbing Mount Everest.

Great is the mind who seeks wisdom.

God gave me something else that I did not understand when it happened, at least, not at first. Words and numbers started to pop into my head when I was worried about things.

Strange words that I had never heard before. First I heard a word. Inside of me, not outside. Then I would hear some numbers, again, inside of me. Sometimes I would hear the same word and different numbers with it. I heard this inside of me. I did not hear audible voices. I heard Inaudibly. I just thought things and knew things inside me. It was all very silent, but it was amazing and so very impressing upon me.

Something was making me want to hunt for the answers!

One day, after having no luck at the library deciding what these odd names and numbers really were, I broke down and asked my husband. Probably in the middle of trying to make a decision having to do with one of my sons or something ... I don't know what ... the object of the worry is not important, just that I again heard an odd word and then numbers.

"John dear, have you ever heard of a word 'calashuns'? Some numbers go with it like 'two two'."

"Are you kidding me? You don't know what that is?"

"No." I cowered through the whack of shame that verbally hit me. "What is it?"

"That's a scripture in the Bible!"

"It is? Oh my gosh! Really?"

"It's the way the Bible says what chapter it is and what verse. Like Colossians chapter two, verse two."

"Oh! I'm supposed to go look up messages in the Bible!"

I ran about the house to locate the old dusty Bible that had been given to me by a girlfriend in high school, the Bible that had moved with me throughout my life time. The Bible that I had never opened or ever read.

Colossians 2:2 = "My purpose is that they may be encouraged in heart and united in love, so that they may have the full riches of complete understanding, in order that they may know the mystery of God, namely Christ ..."

There on the front two pages of my Bible were the words written to me by my girlfriend. I read with awe and fascination Melodee's personal letter to me penned over twenty years earlier. Would that I could ever live up to what she had written in there.

I found the table of contents and nearly came unglued. I started shouting great superlatives of glee and ecstatic amazements!

"Wow! All these words I've been hearing inside me are the names of books in the Bible!"

So it began, or continued, that God did a marvelous thing in me. He inspired me to read from His Bible every time I would hear one of those strange words with the numbers. It took my breath away, and for the first time I knew what the Word of God meant. He inspired this word, I was now quite certain, because when I read one of the "words and numbers" that He told me to go look up (I mean the scriptures and verses) I was inspired to begin to think differently about the situations I was in, and the answers just fell into place.

I got the gift of discernment and I didn't think about it as strange. I just thought this was the best thing since sliced pie.

~~~~~~~~~~

Communions With Christ

CORPUS CHRISTI

Date: April, 1990

There was a slight chill in the air but it was a glorious sunny afternoon when John and I came up over the bridge and entered Corpus Christi. Our son was appearing in a high school band recital that evening and, being good parents who attended our children's school functions, we had followed a caravan of band buses for the seven hour drive.

Coming into view we could see the salt waters of the Gulf of Mexico. I have always loved the ocean. It restores my soul.

We still had four hours before our son's evening concert so John and I drove to a secluded beach area to enjoy the view.

John set up beach chairs, leaned back in his, and fell almost instantly asleep.

I let the sun warm my face.

The symphony of creation was set before my eyes to enjoy. Dancing on the water's edge a delicious medley of great wonder interacted. Beautiful sea shells, tiny burrowing critters finding the sun and hiding — having a buried time under the sand. Tidal patterns coming in and going out. Salty white foaming bubbles leaving delightful shapes. Blue heron and sea gulls swooping down to earth in flight. Faithfully being what they were created to be. Gloriously displaying themselves, decorating my mind with joy.

A strange electricity filled the air.
The hair on my arms stood up in static electricity.
I felt as if an electric surge had entered my awareness.
I could feel someone standing near me.

I sat up on the edge of my chair.
I looked around me.
Other than John I was completely alone on the beach.

The loud squawking of seagulls sounded overhead and behind me.
I turned my face and looked towards the sand dunes.
I saw Raphael standing in the air.
To my utter and complete fright I saw white, the gossamer wonder that is angelic, divinely sent, and meant to talk to me, again.
Raphael was flowing with heat.
The transmitted light that I was allowed to find within my comprehension, with holiness at the helm, took itself and gave shape to an angel of God.
His height — twelve. I do not know what that means, just that I knew he looked 'twelve' in height, or completion of himself, and he was very tall.

It was glorious! Raphael shown out of himself!
Beaming at me, the angel was radiant energy again, resplendent with his countenance. Flowing holy form transmuted to my hardly worthy soul and flowed to my brain as comprehension. **So many things, highly scientific things, gave themselves into my heart and made me find space within me to store these things to be tabulated or addressed at a later time in my life.**

The angel's flowing form was filtered from God's great light. The light was pure and clean. In radiant wonder the light washed the horizon with flowing electrical heat. The radiant energy filled me up with understanding. **A great wave of magnetic energy was washing over my brain. I was being transported into higher**

levels of knowledge, being transported into the higher realms of understanding things.

Divine Voice came into my head with a **bell** like resonance.
Raphael's voice came into me with a resonant **bell** like quality.
I heard the transcendent Tune of Healing.

I sing you the Song, woman. I sing in Victory. I sing holy holy holy.

Jesus Christ the Lamb of God gives out the Proud command to gather for the time has come. I tell you a fortune song. **In song the Lion's whelps gather in prides and find their Father. He sends them out to battle and Praises sing before them.**

Through tongues gathering, and shouting inside their Victory wisdoms, the Song goes out towards the ends of the earth. The Lion of the Tribe of Judah sustains the times and forms the wall of Victory that shuts out the enemy forever. Jesus Christ tells His Pride to stand up and be the warriors who take the times back and make the times your own.

I tell you, women, the rose of Sharon's time has come.

The Archangel then showed me a chart of musical stanzas, empty with no notes upon the lines. Raphael took from the air a flute and played it. Out of the flute (the world cannot make this flute for the flute was a simple God instrument that He made alone) resonances submitted the serenade that peace is. I saw melodies giving shade, and God gave every generation that had gone before and who had loved the Lord with all their hearts the same ability to play in this musical recital of Love. Transmitted from heaven itself divine music sprang out of this flute. Calling ... "Bride, be cheerful! Holy woman, have fun now! Grace is giving you Joy, my Beloved!"

Underneath the flute were hands of many hundreds of people, holding up the heavenly flute, and they played the flute too, and out came funny looking notes. They were not like notes of music I am used to seeing, but I knew they were musical just the same.

Fortune plays the waltz in 4/4 time for you, earth. Open up the ears to hear. Open up the eyes to see. I am Raphael. Lion of Judah

comes ashore to sing you the song of His Bell. Hear with an ear trained by His holy Hand. Take hold of the Note. Learn its Key. Each Note is for you to use, for it is time.
The rose of Sharon's time has come.

Suddenly I saw spiraling notes that emitted a fragrant tune and completed my awareness into knowledge and wisdoms that I never could attain in my own effort. I saw the spiral of notes as a scientific DNA molecular chain within myself and within the universal hearts of mankind. Inside of my inner sight the DNA chain systematically contributed to the formation, and the formation grew healthier. I saw the generations grow stronger in God. I witnessed the invisible realms which spirit takes us into and I spoke with this place, now and in my future years.

Holy. Holy. Holy sang these notes. And God's Victory song was the leader of the tune.

I heard tribulations for myself. I witnessed pain and suffering. I knew that my journey would fill my days with great pain and suffering.

I knew the path of a mystic. I said yes to these times, when asked if I would go on. I was inside of the Holy Trinity of God, speaking to God.

Sharon, fear not what shall come to pass. The God of Israel has sent me to prepare your comprehension. Love in God's light is coming upon you, woman. Then, woman, you will heal.

As Raphael stood eloquently in mid air, hovering with his divine message in his hands to give me, his torso took upon it a sort of blood red vest, like a coat of arms that a soldier in an army would wear to indicate what King he served.

Speaking to me in God language, the angel's torso formed a traditional looking breastplate, golden, with twelve stones inlaid in two rows, six on one side and six on the other side, in a row from top to bottom. The stones rather looked like a ruby, an emerald, a sapphire, an amethyst, a great big diamond, and a garnet, and the last that I was able to identify was Eternal. I just took this stone to be the composite of Eternal. The other stones were to be identified later, God said.

I was aware that when I looked at the angel's breastplate I could see all the way backward in time, or event line, and all the way forward in time or event line of what that thing was that I was seeing in my inner thought and vision.

Raphael held the stems of many different flowers to his heart.

What are those? I spoke inside of my spirit to the angel.

Sharon, the servants of our Lord Jesus stem from the Christ I serve. Flowing is the realm that His servant takes into God's eternal grace. His Love shores you up, and His Buoy takes you through the ship's channels. He is Jesus, the Christ of your salvation. Jesus is here before you now, Sharon. See Him. Open your heart and develop in Christ the way you are chosen to be. His destiny is good. Take the invitation to Life.

Communions With Christ

THE ANGEL'S SONG

Holy Holy Holy. Holy Holy Holy.

Holy Holy Holy. Holy Holy Holy. Holy Holy Holy.

The hair on my arms was standing straight up on end with the strong flow of electricity that enveloped me.
I was sitting on the edge of my beach chair infused with the angel's song.

Holy Holy Holy. Holy Holy Holy.

Randomly I picked up a long piece of driftwood and without thought began to scribble in the sand. I drew meaningless lines and found myself staring at the sand thinking about the majesty that I had just ingested.
Holy holy holy resonated inside of me along with the many things I had digested from a spiritual place.
I was confused. Transported. Reeling with the impact that spiritual communion has upon a person's heart.

Suddenly the stick in my hand began to take possession of His will and this piece of tree drew in the sand. I saw, with my hand holding the stick, with His Hand guiding the lines, that a pair of feet took shape, drawn in the sand upside down to my perspective, so that I was absolutely certain that a pair of holy feet were standing in front of me in the sand on the beach there at Corpus Christi.

The toes pointed towards me.

I knew. But the impact of this knowing was rejected for a moment. Surely not. This cannot be happening to me. Not to me. I am too inconsequential to be having this experience. Yet, I was having this experience. I was Fully taken into His Realms of Mystery.

I slowly got down off my chair and tried to find space to kneel at the feet of Who drew His feet in the sand. I pushed my beach chair back to give me space. I sort of took in the wonderful knowing and I gave myself the permission to surrender to this impossible phenomenon that was truly happening to me.

I kneeled at the feet in front of me. I bowed low towards the toes. I put my head in the sand. I put my forehead in the sand so that only my nose could still catch a breath of air to survive. I bowed before the King.

I knew Jesus was standing invisibly in front of me. Me. Me.

Holy Holy Holy. Holy Holy Holy. Raphael accompanied my recital. It was comforting to know that the angel did not leave, but took position along side this tremendous moment in time for me.

God spoke into my spirit. This was Divine Voice.

My Sharon. I love you, daughter that is my own.

Everything came up. I felt the fatherless wasteland of my childhood in earth. I began to cry uncontrollably. Jesus put His hand on my head in comfort. I cried even more with the recognition of the Father's love, a love I had never ever known on this earth.

Sharon, you are my chosen prophet. The days will be great. The days will be full of pain. I am ready to take you with my Love if you are willing to go on this journey with me.

I hesitantly reached my arm out in front of me, my head still in the sand bowed low in reverence. Still sobbing heart felt releases of emotions with the humble weakness of this encounter I could not believe what I just heard.

As I reached above His feet in the sand my hand touched His burlap robe that was dangling invisibly in front of me, above the feet in the sand. My finger tips slightly touched the hem of the robe that I knew in my spirit took me to places.

I was trembling and sobbing. Overwhelmed with a new sense of reverence to what I was now realizing. Slowly lowering my hand I accidentally brushed my finger tips across the substance of an invisible sandal, in which was the foot that was invisibly Jesus. I could tell that the sandal had traveled far. It felt well worn.

Oh, Lord. Not me. I can't even leave my house without a safe person. I have no ability to be a ... oh Lord, I can't even say the word. It scares me so much. You have the wrong person, Lord. I can't be that. I'm so shy. I fear everything and everyone. There's a lot of things that have to be done by a prophet. I'm not that person, Lord. It is totally beyond possibility for me. Amen.

Dear thing, my word is sufficient to make it the Truth. If you agree, I already have it all worked out, many wonderful things. You are my Prophet. Tell me, would you like to go with me on this journey?

Before I could even get the words out God already knew. I said yes. I thought inside, 'Well, on the other hand, I think I've changed my mind. I want to do this. I will go with You. Yes, Lord'.

Training began.
Jesus began to speak to me. Jesus Christ, the Savior of the world, talked to me — intimately, personally, lovingly and as a Friend, loving me back to health and showing me the way to get home.

I saw a marriage within me. A molecular transformation took place. I contained divine DNA sequencing and I applied these codes to my new state. I was a woman of the church. I

was a mountain of faith. I sold my plot of death to the One who bought my freedom for me.

See your Rose of Great Price sing a Golden Day.

The song of the Trinity placed in my hands opened up and was playing itself in harmony within my mind, and I was at peace and at one with the Maker of the song's words.

I saw seven strings of pearls upon a strand of gold. They shone and were really lovely. Each pearl was separate from the other upon the golden chord and it looked like they were all in the hand of Almighty God.

I am the Lion of the Tribe of Judah who has access to the seven sealed dominions. *The story will be told unto my Bride.*

Christ imprinted me with this awareness.

About this time I noticed that John was now awake. He was sitting up attentively staring at me in amazement!

"I ... I was just talking to God." I stammered trying to re-enter earth's reality.

"I could tell. I could see it on your face." John's serious voice gave confirmation to me.

"Where are we anyway, the Twilight Zone?" Feeling quite stupid and doubtful about John's human receptiveness I tried to brush this experience off with a glib joke.

"No." John spoke pointedly. "We're in Corpus Christi. Do you know what Corpus Christi means?"

"No. What?"

"Corpus Christi means the Body of Christ."

We both sat in reverent silence for quite awhile.
Then I told my husband about the experience.

"Where else would God talk to you except in the Body of Christ?" John's statement was made as he gazed towards the sand dunes and processed the whole occurrence.

~~~~~~~~~

Communions With Christ

SHERMAN

Date: May, 1990

S pring time brings flowers seeded by the Almighty Creator of the majesty of His splendor.

And so it was that on this fine spring morning John and I gathered up a picnic lunch and started to drive north, just meandering our way through some of the back roads of Texas, enjoying the lovely surprises that would come at each new curve in the road. We saw field after field of beautiful bluebonnets — blanketed amongst reds and crimson sheets — like waves they fluttered in the winds and gave their beauty up to our eyes to enjoy the new born flowers of life.

New born colts sired by thoroughbred horses ambled along side their proud mothers. And longhorn steer with many different curls and lengths to their horns grazed in pastures that ranchers tended. John saw a deer sprinting through the brush.

"How about taking that road! Let's go up to Sherman." Directing us by map I swayed us back and forth in country relaxation as the day grew wetter with expectation.

Something was calling me up to Sherman.

"Go that way. Please. I think we are supposed to wind up in Sherman for some reason." It occurred to me to tell John that God was talking to me again.

"Okay by me. It's a nice drive up there."

Just as we entered the city of Sherman a big banner over our heads caught my attention. Hanging over the street, tied with ropes to street poles, was an enormous banner of white tarp with red lettering simply announcing "SHERMAN".

Today God was doing one of His 'dribs and drabs' ways of talking to me. Giving me just enough to get me somewhere, then a little more. I didn't know the full picture. I just obeyed, then I got more information.

I was learning to hear the Holy Spirit's Voice. The way He operates is so fascinating, really impeccable in plan and design. We don't know more than we need to, but just enough to get us to where we are going, on any given day. No overload. Peace, really, if we don't fret and if we believe that God will supply when He is ready to.

"Hey! Let's go in there!" My elation was splashing out of my spirit.

We were passing a beautiful church with colorful stained glass windows. Cars in the parking lot. Something interesting was going on inside. John parked. (The man is nothing if not obliging to me in my emerging butterfly of discovering God.)

A Mass. Catholic. Stately formal church. Wooden pews. Full house. So many people that we sat on the back pew, on the end seats. Great for me. I could watch more cautiously this new and foreign experience for me.

My head peered around the man in front of me to see the priest at the far end of the long isle that led to the alter. He was doing something with white cloths and a plate with something on it and a tall stemmed chalice. The priest had on long white robes with an ornately colored sash or drape that hung about his neck and dropped below the table level out of eyesight.

"What's happening?" I whispered to John, reverently keeping my voice low in respect for the obviously holy service.

"Holy Communion." John was staring ahead. His face looked quite blessed in God's presence.

"What's that?" I really did not know.

"Jesus told everyone to take Holy Communion so they're gunna take the bread and break it. That means His broken body for us. Then the priest will give the cup and that's the blood shed for us."

"Oh." I tried to process this new information.

The priest talked a short while and then people started to get up from their seats and file into a row in the middle isle.

"What's happening now?"

"They're going forward to receive Communion."

I saw what the Lord would call a vision inside of me. I saw the man I was becoming taking communions with Christ, many of them, and then I saw that in the future I would understand these things.

"I'm going up, John." My voice still whispered the sentence while my body rose and got in line with the other people going to the alter for Communion.

"You can't go! You're soul isn't right with God. You're not Catholic." John grabbed my hand and tried to pull me back to sit down and behave myself.

"I'm going. Jesus is calling me to come to Him and take His Communions with Him."

I had never taken Holy Communion before in my life. I had no idea that any such ritual or command was performed or expected or ..... God as my witness ... all I can say is that at this time in my life ... truly I did not understand this new thing.

Him Self took me Up with Him in Spirit. That is All I need.

Nothing could keep me from going forward. God was shouting inside of me, *"Come into my Communions with me Christ."*

Red crimson floating about my inner man, golden rays indelibly tanking my hands with the inks of fortune, pressing my bones into Godly hues, juggling my days with care, fighting in my mind, floating past the days, allowing this process, being in Communions With Christ, swimming great laps in the salt that wet my opera, having Him be the Guide.

I went up. I took Holy Communion In The Christ that talked with me and led me to know His ways.

As I walked back to my wooden pew I heard the strangest message from the Lord inside of my spirit.

Take Notes. I am going to sheer you, my sheep. I love your long wool, Lincoln. I am the sheep Shearer and I am having a lovely time trimming your fleece to be just the right length to hold your shape.

... Jesus said to me I will 'sheer' you, and I understood this in my mind to mean ... like make me 'sheer' as if I was operating apart from anything else and becoming just the song He was making me, and that this 'sheering' would make me climb up a perpendicular mountainside to get to my heights in a holy vessel that was being trimmed newly to take upon myself a grand appearance inside of me. I knew this process of sheering was the same for all who follow Jesus. It is the process from which He allows us to become completely altogether in Him. Amen.
... Jesus said to me that He is 'the sheep Shearer', and this I took in my spirit to mean that He trims away that which does not meet His expectations for our appearance in Him.

"SHERMAN". The Banner over our heads read SHERMAN as we drove out of town, the same banner that was over our heads when we drove in to town.
It occurred to me to look up the meaning of that word some weeks later, having had time to mull over my God experience. My shock can only match the extremely intricate tapestry of miracles that God is putting together for me to witness.

Sherman means: Shearer. One who shears sheep.

Communions With Christ

WHITE FALCONER

Long ago, when I was ignorant of God's ways, I did not understand the symbolism behind many things that the Lord sent to me in mysterious wisdoms. I did, however, know that they called me deeper into the yearnings to understand the entire picture, or, at least, to know the One who was sending me these things to have and to hold forever more.

Date: June, 1990

The gulf waters crashed on the sea wall rocks beneath the pier that I stood upon in the early morning sunshine, the waves making their sounds so poignant to me because I knew I was leaving all this beauty.

It was the last day of our vacation. The morning after I had sat in Galveston's finest seafood restaurant and dined upon crab-au-gratin, the morning after I had taken the dinner rolls and the crackers from the table and stuffed them into my purse and my pockets.

I wanted to feed the birds.

It just came to me as I was eating. I needed to feed the birds. The birds needed feeding. I was called to feed them.

It seemed such a strange and foreign voice, the little thing that talked into me.

Spiritual nudgings? I was hearing something, and it was part of the mysteries.

The next morning, while my husband was inside the Flagship Inn paying our hotel bill and taking our luggage to our car for the drive home, I had broken away and gone out onto the pier over the sea wall breakwaters. The mere water's pull was something that I could not take home with me and I so longed to see it all one more time.

For one last moment. Sensing and smelling the wonders — searching the horizons of the salt water that drew me to love it so much. Breathing in the sky's blue majesty.

My hands reached into my paper napkin, which was folded over last night's dinner rolls, and I began breaking off the bread.

I saw the sea gulls start to swoop down for their bread, and so, I threw the birds their bread, piece by piece, heavenward. Up. Over my imagination and beyond my dreams. Into a miracle that was about to happen to me.

The wings of the gulls over my head were like a canopy of love. Their squawking voices a tender serenade to me. My son came out onto the pier for a few moments. He snapped a photograph of me feeding the birds before he went back into the hotel to help his dad.

It was a glorious moment. Seagulls swooping down to grab a bite. I threw the bread up to the birds soaring freely in flight above me.

I fed the birds.

In watching their flight patterns I was suddenly aware of a wonderful thing. The sea gulls' eyes targeted the bread so easily and they were able to zero in on their target and take and eat. The birds soared when they caught their bread. Some gulls were shy, or too fearful to swoop towards the bread, and they did not get to eat. Why? It teased me and took my soul into a knowing. I was shy. I missed out the bread of life that had been thrown at me for years, I missed out the meal. Why?

I thought about the old sign we see every time we drive into Galveston. Painted on the side of an old church, welcoming us, the sign boldly reads "God's Love Is On This Island."

I felt the morning heartbeat that is the Love of God.

Something nudged my heart and so I obeyed. I turned towards the clear blue skies and looked at the spot that called me.

What radiance! Was the sun blinding me?

I saw open skies toward heaven splitting and revealing the glory of their places. I saw white. It became clearer and clearer. Who was that?

I saw a figure in glorious splendor filtering out of the split skies, out of the rather wonderful revelation that I was in the middle of and did not know it yet.

Justice came out of the skies.

He was a White Falconer. I saw a man's figure, as if husbandry wanted to plant a seed within my brain, a seed of great wealth to vaporize within the atmosphere that I lived within, to take root and then take shape and flesh itself out in my life.

If only I would have known then the whole picture, but the snapshot was still developing.

Your Majesty? Your Elegance? Your Grace?

I didn't know what to address the figure as.

Justice and Grace and Elegance and Majesty were what I saw.

No name was given to me to know Him by other than that He was a very high priest. And then He showed me Himself as a figure that took the shape of a White Falconer.

(Father, forgive me for not knowing the perfectly radiant presence of Yourself, for not knowing You. However, I now realize that knowing You is a series of openings that You allow us to travel into, or doors that we take if we choose to follow Your invitation, or trips that you give us into Holy places, and from these we take souvenirs, and these are indelible snapshots that develop. I see now, Jesus, that You develop.)

Jesus develops.

Like a photograph in the ink, we come into a clearer image all the time. Let my snapshot bear Your image, Lord God, I pray. Give me deeper and deeper wisdoms and radiance into Your countenance.

Yet I think if we were to face You all at once the power of the revelation would flat line us. I'm just speculating. And if we went flat line by truly seeing You then I think You would have already taken us into heaven to be at Your side. But, I regress, and so let me continue with my testimony to Your romantic wooing of me into loving You, Lord God.

I saw a White Falconer. Radiant. A vision for certain. In the skies high over Galveston Bay, above the salt water. And I was mesmerized by the vision for it was taking my soul into the mysteries that I so longed to meet and to live by.

In this vision the White Great Falconer was floating in the sky, serene and peaceful, very certain of Himself, and quite calm. He was holding His arm out. His arm was carrying birds upon it. These things that looked like birds were His birds of prey and when He loosed them to go forth they returned with the target that He had sent the birds out to retrieve for Him.

In holy vision there is symbolism. I just did not know that then.

I witnessed a very divine symbolism there in the morning light of my dawning awakening, my awakening to the works of the Lord.

His arm was fearless and His height was tall. I saw the bird He loosed fly in towards the land. I saw the bird fly out of my sight, but I knew that the bird would come back, because the bird was the White Falconer's and no where else would do to live but the place of resting within the sanctuary of His arm and His care.

It made little sense to me then. I am just recounting it now, as the event took place, even though I was totally ignorant — the pieces of the puzzle of God's mystery still forming themselves and not yet fitting into the finished mosaic of knowledge within my wee brain. What took me quite by surprise and stained my heart forever through a holy process, the ink being made quite fine and written into my spirit as Truth, what had such an impact upon me that I have pondered this event these many years, has taken so many years to be able to put into human words. Though I knew it then, the Person and the Event I mean, all remembered exactly, I did not know the

Holy Spirit's ways of communicating, and so, I just thought I had seen a miracle, and heard a very strange and perplexing thing within my heart.

I was one of the White Falconer's birds — and I needed fixing.

I saw within my vision that the White Falconer was fixing up these birds, that came to His arm and rested there with Him. I mean fixing.

I saw him fix this bird, the bird that I am, as well as I saw Him fix other birds, too. I saw Him make the bird that was me all well enough to fly forth bravely, out to see what I was sent out to get, so that I could reach my target thing and then return to be fixed some more. I saw each bird take flight that returned to His Arm.

And I knew that I would return to His arm, too, where He would feed me and care for me ... going and getting the wisdom that was each morsel of bread that I took as communion in Him.

And so I flew, by my own free will, up into the skies over Galveston bay, and landed upon the arm of the White Falconer. And I saw better what He was looking at, for my perspective of all things had shifted by being at His heights.

I was then sent out into the lands. There were targets that I was supposed to go to, and He made me know just how to fly to each target, and He gave me the power to bring the target back to Him. And we together, the target retrieved by His directions to me, and myself ... landed upon His arm. And there we were, this White Falconer and myself quite at one with the perfect peace of His countenance, communing privately within this mystery.

May I interject here that as soon as I flew back and landed with His prized prey that He had sent me out to return to Him, I was extremely aware that I was greatly in a state of His overwhelming love covering me. His Hand showed me more fixings. In this state I did not see the other bird of prey which I had carried by my mouth towards the Falconer in the sky because he, the other bird, was in some other private mansion with God.

I saw a miracle. I saw the entire process of the Christian witnessing and finding of lost things and bringing them to Christ.

All of these things ... people, situations, voices, hearts, purposes, days, and nights lost in tears. I saw it all in a vision. Symbolic and awesome. My soul was allowed to see this before I ever understood what it all meant.

God's gift to me of His heavenly vision means so much to me for the simple reason that it came to me at a time in my walk when I truly was absolutely as green and ignorant as a door post — my mind a total blank — devoid of any of the doctrines and beliefs of Christianity.

In the after mass of looking back on the whole event I can say to you that in future years I was floored with weeping joy when I finally understood in my deep levels of spirit that God had truly spoken to me and showed me His immeasurable mystery and love for us all.

~~~~~~~~~~

Colossians 3:1-4 *"Since, then, you have been raised with Christ, set your hearts on things above, where Christ is seated at the right hand of God. Set your mind on things above, not earthly things. For you died, and your life is now hidden with Christ in God. When Christ, who is your life appears, then you also will appear with him in glory."*

KNOWINGS - GOD'S GIFTS

Fortune.
I did not recognize what the package was that the Lord gave to me. I satisfied myself with the knowledge that I just knew things that I should not really know.

I had knowings. However, these knowings were not, at the time, associated in my mind with any gifts from God. I did not know anything about spiritual giftings.

I just was a wreck of misunderstanding and had for the life of me no idea that I was being given spiritual giftings. I just knew that something very odd was happening to me.

I kind of knew things that I should not have any way of knowing.

Still at Galveston ...

It took God no time at all to demonstrate His powers within my evolving spiritual awakening. The words come to me now, but back then I would have called myself a terribly mixed up woman experiencing some frightening and amazing occurrences that made me question my very sanity.

I wanted to keep this secret because being odd was being crazy. I had enough shame and guilt heaped on me during my childhood. I didn't want the shame or guilt of being 'nuts' as well as agoraphobic and riddled with terrible anxieties that kept me barely functioning in life. I was shell shocked from the trauma of my youth and I held onto my poor woe begotten identity for dear life. No one was going to shake my pity party from my ingrained depressed way of looking at things. I was comfortable this way.

But ... I knew something was going on.
I had just seen a vision of a White Falconer.

I walked up to the check out desk of the Flagship Inn where John was leaning on one elbow having a chat with the check out clerk. All I could think of was getting my husband's attention to tell him about my vision when suddenly my attention was riveted upon the golden necklace around the throat of the clerk behind the reservations desk.

Her brown skin highlighted with splendor this golden braided chain, rather tight about her neck. I stared at this thing. It was speaking to me. I mean, seeing the necklace gave me wisdoms. I should not have known these knowings, but they came to me anyway.

"Have ... have you ..." I stammered. Trying to work up the nerve to verify what I knew inside. I could not bring myself to say the sight I saw. It troubled my inner heart so deeply. Tragedy. Pain. Loss of childhood. Agony, betrayal. Violation. Internal malicious devil of torment rising up to show me the face of sin. I saw sin. Oh how my time and eyes were taken to the very heart of the sin of man and the terrible torment that comes from its results to the innocent victims of sin.

I said what the spirit told me to say. Of course I did not know this was the Spirit. I just sort of tried to find the words.

"I know your son loved you very much." I said this with deep emotion, brimming with my tears of understanding from the depth of Truth, to the startled eyes of the clerk as her face turned to hear my words of kindness. A healing balm came up and out of my mouth, out to the ready thoughts and mind of the reservations clerk with the golden necklace about her throat, words that told her the thing she longed to hear. Words that brought life back to a dead place. Order to a universe that had been only pain.

The tears formed in my eyes. Tears from my own pain, mingled with her pain. I saw the sin. And my own past torments from sins against me came up within me and brought the tears up to the brim of my seer's eyes. And I told her that her son loved her.

Love is such a needed thing, in all of us. When we lose the love we need, we are empty. I felt her terrible emptiness when I looked at the golden necklace around her throat.

I saw the tears begin to form in her eyes, too.

I knew. She knew I knew.

It was a riveting moment between us as souls that the same Creator made.

"My son died in a drive by shooting," she said. "He was only sixteen years old when he died in a pool of his own blood. I heard the gun shot, but by the time I came out of the house he was already dead. The car was driving away." With that comment she clasped her hand to her necklace. She did not stop staring at me because she knew that I knew, and the depth of this experience was healing to her somehow.

"He gave me this necklace for my birthday the week before he was murdered," she said.

And then she held her head a little higher, and with a renewed resolve she said with great peace and dignity, "Thank you."

All I could do was sort of nod my head in confirmation that I knew the depths of sin's great loss to its victims. I had to walk away. I parted from her and never saw her again. But we had communicated with the language that transcends all words.

We exchanged a little kindness in place of the horrible pain that we each knew.

QUESTIONS

Date: Summer 1990 and Onward ....

How can I answer these things? I am totally without religious training. I have no friends who go to church. In fact, I have no friends.

Do not worry. I will give you what you need each day. Sustenance shall come as you need the sustenance and you will come to know. Be Strong. Have Courage.

I was already talking with God as if He was standing right there with me and we were just having an intimate little chat between best buddies. I heard His Voice.

Just the mere awakening from God had so revitalized my quest for life that I wanted to go hunt for the answers. There were so many puzzling details to my mystical experiences. This was obviously God's plan, of course! Not to tell me every answer to His mysteries all at once so that I would go search out the answers, in the days we walk together.

What value is a thing if we never really search for or know without any doubt that our quest has exhausted all possibilities and we finally hold in our hand the True Treasure?

I wasn't wise enough then to catch on to the healing process going on. I didn't understand about the renewing of the mind. God certainly did use the curiosity He put into me to start the healing of the phobias I hung on to.

Our family had no computer. The internet was hardly even an invention then.

If I wanted any answers I was forced to gather up my courage and leave my house alone! I had to drive all the way to the library, get out of my car, walk in, and then search out holiness amongst a room full of strangers! Hugely difficult for me. Very frustrating. Many of the large reference books that God sent me to read could not be checked out!

But, God led me to every book I needed! It was supernatural!

I would have a question. Or God would put the question in my mind and just allow me to think I had a question, so He could lead me to the answer. God knew every question I had whether or not I openly articulated them. It could be just a passing thought one morning, a fleeting glimmer that hardly registered in me some afternoon, and there I would be an hour later driving to the library, being led by God Almighty to a certain isle and to a certain book. Then I would 'know' this was the book with the answer. Then I would take the book off the shelf. I would run my hand outside of the cover, up and down. It felt to me like God was imprinting the contents of the book into my DNA somehow.

Then God would tell me the page to open the book to, or God literally caused my hand to open the book to the exact page I needed without my participation in this gesture at all! Then God would have my eyes fall upon the exact sentence or paragraphs of information I needed. Then I would read.

He gave me Seer's eyes. Then immediately I was whisked away 'up'. Up in the Spirit. Soaking up the mysteries and higher thoughts of God as seen through the eyes He gave me to see with. He took me up with Him. Up into the revelatory regions where God did a supreme thing. He made me love Him. He made me appreciate the heavenly realm. I know this realm as well as I know this earth because I have gone there so many times with God!

Hundreds of questions. Thousands of answers. It really did expedite time for God to lead me to the very answer He wanted me to know without waste of time.

I was in training.

God's training of my mind covered a tremendous amount that was infilled to me with rapid and supernatural capacity and velocity. Kinetics played a part in these times. I suddenly was a vessel of growth. And God, watering my mind, would take me into His gardens and pick the flowers of Truth and plant them into my soul. His Hand being the Master Gardner made this garden a healthy one in me.

I was not really led to study any books that God did not tell me to look at. I was listening to the Honorable Teacher of The Truth and He was doing a God job in me.

I remember that I did not want to listen to anyone else because I was suspect that I might pick up some human train of thought and get confused from the Holy train of thought that was indwelling within me The Lord's Life. I was in Love and Love took me to my healing, Himself. He gave me dreams and visions. Daily for at least a year I dreamed and then I woke and then I asked God the dreams' meanings and He told me. I wrote these things down. In God's language. He used the most amazing great symbolisms and parables and fun stories. He would make me laugh and make me cry and make eternity understandable for me.

We together went to find the answers. I was taken out of my agoraphobia and out of my claustrophobia and into the place where the really happy people live in earth's joy.

He was not sparing me any troubles.

Part of the training was suffering, and I suffered tremendously.

I was very angry with God at all the suffering I endured. But even though I felt my whole life had been suffering there was more to come. It took me awhile to get in stride, and I tried every day to obey. I heard my Healer's Voice talking with me, telling me everything pertaining to my own personal journey that I needed to know, and we got more well together. He is my Great Physician. For the record He is the God that Heals. He took my haunted spirit and woke the place up from the dead zone. He chased the spooks and demons away. It was a fierce job. We still work together in these fields, when ever attack comes against the place of Joy that God wishes us each to live in.

Mystical songs of God.
My ears heard notes.

Without fail I got goose bumps, the hair on my arms stood up like an electrical charge was going through me. I felt faint. I swooned. I was taken up into revelatory regions of comprehension. The world got smaller and heaven got huge. And I simply understood what the mystery was that God was showing me at any given moment in my training. It was no longer a mystery because the Lord had supplied me with natural understanding of Godly ways.

We are all so ignorant that we do not know that the natural way to live is in the presence of God — talking to Him face to face. He is a good friend who will explain His mind to us and give us the most amazing information. Doesn't a good friend tell you what's going on in his life and how things work that he is working on and that sort of thing?

One day in the library I found out that 'David's' Lord refers to the 'David' in the Christian Bible. I read that David was a King and also a type and shadow of the coming Christ, and that Jesus Christ came from the lineage and the house of David. So it made perfect sense to me that Raphael would introduce himself to me by saying *I am an angel of David's Lord.* I could always hold on to that to know with certainty that I was truly having a God experience.

I was having a gigantic God experience! Every day the experience got bigger and more complex. More mysteries revealed. More supernatural occurrences. More questions. More answers. More questions. More growth.

I was in training by God Himself!

When the Archangel Raphael appeared to me I saw a breastplate with twelve stones and I could see all the way backwards and all the way forwards. God led me to the knowledge of the Old Testament being a forerunner of Christ that looks backwards, and Jesus Christ being the New Covenant that looks forward. God also told me He meant this as a revelation that I was a Seer and would be seeing future things as well as former things by the spirit.

When I saw the angel I knew by the Spirit that one of the stones on Raphael's breastplate was an 'amethyst' stone which looked sort of transparently violet in color and texture.

Quite a long time after seeing the angel Raphael's breastplate I read this: "In the Bible an amethyst is worn on the breastplate of Aaron, the high priest of the Hebrews, who was filled with the desire to please God and who had the gift of tongues."

Happy discoveries like this, for example, would make me investigate and read about who Aaron was. Reading about Aaron would then fill me with questions which would lead me to more readings about other people in the Bible.

One day I looked up what was meant by 'the gift of tongues'.
Now this disturbed me!

I can distinctly remember saying with firmness to God, "Now look here God! I appreciate You speaking to me and all. But this is working well enough with us speaking face to face so clearly to each other. I don't want to speak in a bunch of gibberish that no one can understand and I can't understand. In fact, I refuse. That's my one really serious request of You so far, God. I won't have it. If You're going to talk to me, God, then communicate with me in a clear language so I clearly understand what You're saying. I feel very strongly about this, God. No gibberish. You talk to me clearly, and I'll talk to You clearly. Okay?"

God replied, *"Love has no bounds and so it shall be unto you as you ask."*

Okay. I was quite immature then.
God is really never told what to do by mortals.
I later realized that He was planning all along to talk to me quite clearly. His love is so polite.

He did always talk to me quite clearly. I could hear every word of the Voice of God quite clearly. I mean, when I bothered to listen.

However, I did not always clearly understand the meaning of what He clearly said.

And clearly I forgot to ever listen to Him at all on several occasions, like, to my dismay.

If only we would listen to God's symphony, the one He has played at us since our very birth.

SEEDS

Year: 1992

It was early days when God was speaking to me. I was still trying to distinguish the Voice of God from the din of the world. True, God had personally told me He was going to talk to me. But I was a very young sheep, trying to figure out the language of my Shepherd.

One day, on our way home from a nice day's outing, we were driving through downtown Fort Worth and passed a sullen looking psychic and horoscope shop with bars in the windows. I heard the Lord speak.

Go in there.

I let John keep driving. It terrified me.

I am with you. Be strong.

"John, I'm supposed to go in that psychic shop back there. Can we turn around?"

"No. We're not supposed to have anything to do with that stuff."

"But ... God. God just told me to go in there."

John turned our car around in the middle of the road and parked directly in front of the den of satan. Then he stared at me.

I entered very cautiously. Massive anxiety welling up within me.

God kept nudging me forward. It was quite unnerving to me to be surrounded by rows of books on witchcraft, horoscopes, spells, and satan. My skin crawled. My spirit took umbrage and wretched inside. I was in the enemy's camp. Alone.

I am with you, Sharon. Have courage. Go over there.

Displays of geological rocks, crystals, and geodes were all labeled with their types, and priced to sell. In the center was a raised pedestal covered in black silk with a large crystal ball and a few quartz strategically placed about.

I remembered the days of my youth. I had been raised by a tormenting father who was by trade a geologist. The very sight of geological specimens took my heart to a place I did not treat with kindness in my memory bank. I hated rocks.

Oh Lord! What are you doing? I cried out to Jesus for assistance.

I saw three teenaged boys dressed in goth black looking for something. They circled the rocks and finally asked the sales clerk a question.

Go listen.

I scooched a little closer, trying not to seem obvious, so that I could hear.

I saw John waiting at the doorway with his arms folded. He was not coming in.

"Hey dude, what's the name uv the rock that takes away negative energy? I've got like tons uh bad karma messing with me, man."

"We no got that."

"Like tell me the name uv the rock 'n I'll go somewhere else. I gotta get this negative crap offa me."

"I tell you we no got that."

"You stupid jerk. You call this a rock shop? You got a spell 'r somethin'?"

"You go look." The shop keeper motioned towards the books on spells.

"Whatta waste uv time. Let's get outta here, man."

Suddenly I knew. I heard a revelation. I heard a theological fact and a true revelation from the true God. From these boys' God. From my God. From our God. We were all lost and looking for the answers. It just took different turns and different twists, but those boys were myself. I was them. Searching. I knew that we are here on this earth to help each other to know the Truth to our questions.

But of course I was stuck in my flesh. My flesh was stuck in my habitual anxiety responses to things. And so the three goth boys brushed past my husband and out the door while I just stood there like an idiot.

I knew the name of the rock!

I don't know whether I wanted to get out of that shop more or catch up with the three boys before they got away, but I sprinted to the entry and saw them about to cross the street. They were stopped at a red light.

"Hey! I know the name of the rock that takes away negative energy!" I waved my arm as they looked at me.

The negative energy boy approached me. "What?"

The name of the Rock that takes away negative energy is Jesus!" I smiled.

"A Jesus freak."

The most amazing information came up out of me. My testimony came out in words he would understand about the abusive childhood I had, and the visits by an angel, and then God appearing to me, and Jesus being real if you ask Him to save you from the darkness of oppression and negative energy.

"I'll think about it." The goth boy crossed the street. He had listened through three light changes before leaving.

I was angry. I had such a good conversation going that I wanted to lead my first person to accept Jesus, notch my belt, snap my invisible suspenders on my puffed up chest, rock back on my heels with pride — and he just walked off from me!

Hey, God! I obeyed! And I went into that horrible shop and talked to that kid and told him the revelation, and I told him about You. How come I didn't get to lead him to Christ? Huh?

God very clearly said in my spirit ...

You do not always get to see the flower bloom. Sometimes you are sowing seeds.

~~~~~~~~~

Communions With Christ

DAVID AND JOB

Date: 1992

One day while I was pumping my own gasoline at a neighborhood gas station, a feat that made me quite proud of my progress because at the age of forty something I finally stopped making my husband do this task and learned how to do it myself, healing was taking place.

Go tell that guy ...

God directed my head to look up. God made me 'see' a man pumping gas at the next bay.
No God! I won't! Don't make me talk to *him*! He's too scary looking. He's so greasy. And dirty. He has long hair. And bad teeth. He's not my type of person at all, as You well know, God!
I gave the Lord my excuse list like it mattered to God. I was out of my comfort level once again! That's the way God stretched me at the most unexpected times. It was really most inconvenient and quite annoying to me!

Go tell that guy that I AM his Lord and that I say that I am David's Lord. Tell him to remember this scripture ...

I will not! You can't be serious, God! I would never ever in my life speak to a filthy person like that! Yuk!

I was frozen. Do I obey? Or not obey? That is the question.

The man got in his dirty beat up old truck and turned on the engine.

There was still time.

I did nothing. He started to drive away.

No! NO!

My leg took one step towards the truck so that God would think I was making an effort. My arm kinda waved a teensy flap and my wrist flopped down "you there ... stop". Did God believe me? Was I convincing enough that I had tried? But, hey, it's not my fault that the guy didn't hear me and drove off! I thought so.

Good cover, Sharon.

With great relief I watched the truck get out of hearing range. Then. Suddenly. Where did that come from? A sign on the side of the truck appeared. A lawn service company name with a phone number. A magnetic sign on the door panel beneath the driver hanging his mud covered elbow out his rolled down truck window.

Did you do that God? To help me obey?

I wrote down the company's name and phone number on a scrap of paper from the floorboard of my car. I wrote down the guy's scripture and his message exactly as I heard it from God. I would mull it over.

Should I deliver the guy's message? Maybe I would. Maybe I wouldn't.

I drove home slowly. Wrestling with God. How could I go from being so proud of myself for pumping gas to being so disappointed in myself for not obeying God?

Father, should I do it?

It would make a big difference in the young man's life.

The company's name was in our local phone book. There was the address. The phone number matched. It must be him.

I devised a plan.

I would just write his message on a piece of paper and explain the situation in writing. I would deliver this written note to the man's work address and give it to the receptionist. Then I would not have to talk to this horrid person. I would put my name and phone number in the note in case he wanted to call me to thank me or tell me how wonderful I was to be hearing God. Yeah, that would make me feel real good.

Okay.

My note was ready. I got in my car. The address was not far away at all. Arriving gave the willies a small run for their money when I saw a dilapidated old house and the man's truck in the dirt driveway. A dog barking near the fence stood on old tires then ran back and forth ferociously between debris strewn about the dying grass.

Where was the company? Where was the receptionist?

Euuuww. Fear and Flight. Terror. Repulsion. It looked the very poorest of conditions. This was his personal home!

Steadily ... slowly ... I clumped my lead legs up the front sidewalk, step by labored step, watching, so as not to slip a shoe into the cavernous dirt cracks in the aged cement and break an ankle. About twelve centuries later I arrived at the screened door.

Squeeeeek. Squeeeeek. The slower I tried to open the door the more the old thing squeeked.

The rolled note in my sweaty palm slipped right inside the paintless wooden door's handle. No need to knock. Just gotta get away before someone opens the door. Just gotta concentrate on my car now. Why is my car seven miles away? Clump. Clump. Anxiety gives me dead legs.

The next day my phone rang.

"Rose! It's me, David! You're a prophet! You're a prophet of God! I got your note!" The man was shrieking with a non stop high pitched jubilation. "You know that scripture God told you to tell me? That's the scripture that made me accept Jesus Christ as my Savior! I used to say it every night in my prayers before I went to sleep! But I've been kinda backslidden lately. Rose! You're a prophet of God! No one but a prophet of God could have know that scripture! Rose! I'm David! Your note said God told you to tell me He is David's Lord! I'm David! He's my Lord! I've been backslidden and God sent you to tell me my scripture again and He's David's Lord. I'd better not be backslidden because He's my Lord! I'm David! You're a prophet! You are incredible! You should be on TV! It's a miracle! How do you do that? Can I meet you?"

Okay, Lord. I get it. Please make him stop shouting these things over and over at me. I'm embarrassed for my pridefullness. I get the point. I left my phone number in the note so it could be all about me. I wanted a thank you. I wanted the guy to go wild and praise me. But it's about You, God, right? I'm sorry, Lord. I repent. Please forgive me.

Holy Sharon, your gift is from my Hand. I love your journey. I know that you never heard praises growing up. I give you praises because you need them so badly. You have great value to everyone. I give you a bouquet of roses and praises go forth before you. You are my Prophet. Some will recognize and tell you they know.

He develops. Jesus develops. He really develops. Your journey and my journey are all about the development that character is. I was slow. Selfish. Needy of praise. I got none as a child. God knew that. He let me get some all out shouting praise and Halleluiahs. He loves us while He teaches us humility. It's a strange mixture of God growth. We get the Master's song and find our way in the notes.

The man began to call me every day. For a few days God gave me wisdoms to council the man, who was indeed backslidden and had many problems. We talked only by telephone. I would not allow him to come to my home. But then it became obvious to me that he was starting to worship my giftings and not worship Jesus who had given us all these wonderful things. So I told him to stop calling and follow Jesus.

A few days later David was standing at my front door yelling "Rose! Come out! I know you're in there! Rose! God sent me over here to tell you something!"

He was quite excited. He had a Bible in his hands, waving it in the air. No matter how long I hid in my house peeking out of my window at him he would not stop yelling, "Rose. Open the door! God sent me here to tell you something!"

Finally I opened the door.

We sat on my front deck under the stately oak tree's shade.

"God told me to read you the story of Job!"

"Who is Job?"

"You never heard of Job?"

"No. Who is he?"

"He's a guy in the Bible. Cool! I get to read you the story of Job for your first time to hear it!"

I found out who Job was.

David read scriptures out loud with great enthusiasm. And somewhere in the middle of the story God let me know His message.

My hand clasped at my heart with great fear.

God was telling me that I was coming into a time of great tribulations, boils and sores or something awful, and trials that would cause any man to turn from God.

I was terribly afraid. And David kept on reading the Bible to me, quite unaware of my inner knowings.

Sharon, promise me that you will never leave me or ever stop loving me.

I promise Lord. What is going to happen to me?

Sharon, promise me that you will never leave me or ever stop loving me.

I promise Lord. This is scaring me.

Sharon, promise me that you will never leave me or ever stop loving me.

I promise Lord. I promise.

David finished his scripture reading and went home.

Job never turned from God no matter how many of his friends advised him to curse God for his miserable plight. What great love for God. What great inner strength Job must have had.

Three times the Lord made me promise Him that I would never leave Him or ever stop loving Him. It was a gravely serious request from God, that promise.
He meant the promise to help me. I knew that.

A week later I found the lump under my left arm.
I was diagnosed with breast cancer. It had spread into my lymph nodes.
If God had not made me promise Him that I would never leave Him or ever stop loving Him, I would have. I was so angry with God for allowing me to suffer so much.
But I had promised God, and I could never break my promise.
The promise He made me give to Him saved my life.

GOD'S SAVING GRACE

God is good. Loving. Healing. And Saving. Saving even of sinners found out by themselves to be in an unfixable situation. I think the Lord loves us even enough to come seek us out at the darkest moment there is of our lives and try to make us listen. Holy. I think God is magnificent, the holy is divine, and His wisdom is immaculate.

Year: 1993

Fortunately, God does speak to us. Sometimes He takes a rather unique and round about way of doing so. Sometimes He uses someone else to deliver us a message. But, God does speak. Lovingly He speaks to us, His flock.

"You can't order!"
John had his menu open and his mouth too, about to tell the waiter his desires for lunch.
"Why?"
"I can't eat here!"
I stood up and began to walk out of the restaurant muttering 'sorry' to the confused waiter standing there watching our swift exit. John's face looked extremely miffed. It wasn't until we hit the parking lot that I felt free enough to say that God was talking to me again.
"Just where the heck does God say we can eat?" John is addicted to food.

"Look, I don't always get the whole message right at the same time. I just get little dribs and drabs of words or impressions. If I obey I might get a little more, okay!"

We walked across the parking lot to an Italian place, even though I knew we were not going to stay there either. I was just biding time because God had not told me any more yet.

"I'll have the ... " John's stomach was readying itself for shrimp.

"Excuse me! We can't eat here either!" I looked apologetically at the waitress and slid my heavy wooden chair back to get out fast. John slammed his menu down on the table with an irritated thud.

We stood in the parking lot again. I could hear John's stomach rumbling with hunger.

"So? Where does God say we can eat?" If sarcasm and unbelief could be personified with a sound it would be the sound of my husband's voice at that moment.

"I don't know." I really did not know. I just knew that my husband was very mad at me for ruining his lunch.

It takes a lot, to say the least, quite a lot of courage to obey God even when the person we are with is very put out that he is inconvenienced. I have to say it took a supreme amount. To look back on it and tell the story now, it took all the faith I could muster up to obey and believe that I was really hearing God — to so disorganize our human day's schedule this way, and to cause a fight. The human reaction to the inconvenience was immense.

John gunned the accelerator. I lurched in my passenger seat.

"God better hurry up and speak or the car will just run into that building."

"Drive that way! Go west on the freeway." I did not hear God say anything. I just sort of discerned that was the way to go.

"Take a left. I mean exit here and then turn left at the first street." I was leaning forward in my chair, peering out the car windshield but looking into the future of someone. Fortunately God was giving me enough to guide me, even though I had no idea where I was going or why. I just listened and followed His Voice.

Communions With Christ

John was still mad when we passed the row of fast food restaurants. His hands clenched the steering wheel.

"There! That's it! That's where we're supposed to be!"

John swung our car into a parking space at a slimy looking fast food restaurant and braked just before hopping the curb.

"Can I at least eat here?" John asked.

"I think so." How wonderful to talk to God, yet how irritating to be the one who has to wait with someone who talks to God.

We went in.

Nothing. I got nothing. God said nothing. I heard nothing.

John was already at the counter ordering a tray of food. I ordered, too.

We took our food to a booth. I wiped the grease off the table top, and the seat. We sat down. John began shoveling his food into his mouth. I began looking around for someone to appear with a magic halo over their head or a radiant star or something to point them out to me. But nothing. Not a sign. Zip. Nada. Nil. Zero.

I put a tiny bite of mashed potatoes in my mouth.

A man walked in. By himself. Dressed in a suit. He did not order any food.

It was him. I did not know it at first because God did not tell me right away. God just had me sort of rivet my attention towards the man with what must have been an impolite stare that never took my eyes off the man.

He sat down at a table by himself. Folded his hands. Stared straight ahead.

He could very well have been waiting for someone. But he wasn't. God brought him in there. God brought me in there. To talk to him. So, I guess really the man was waiting for me, but he didn't know it yet.

Go tell him that I said I am hearing his prayers and not to do the thing he is planning to do today.

What God!

I said, go tell

I heard you Lord! I mean no! I can't. He'll think I'm crazy!
God was silent. Just waiting. He had spoken. I had heard. My turn.

"John, psssst!" I actually leaned in across the booth and psssssst my husband to get his attention. I was sweating with anxiety. A hot flush of fear had popped up all over me.
"God is telling me to go tell that man something. I can't! I'm having an anxiety attack!"
"No you're not. Go tell him." John cared more about his mouth full of liver and gizzards than my plight.
I got up from the booth ... walked towards the man. Passed right by him and entered the women's restroom. There, that looked smooth! No one will ever notice.
"Help me, God!" I spoke out loud to the reflection of my sweaty forehead and ashen grey face in the bathroom mirror.
Silence. Nothing.
I was in the stall when it occurred to me that the man might get up and leave before I could tell him his God message so I washed up fast and ran out into the restaurant.
He was still there. Okay. Now or never. Just do it.
I pulled out the chair across from him at his table and dropped down onto it sideways because my legs were becoming noodles of jelly. I sat down at this man's table, uninvited!
"Excuse me. God told me to come tell you something." I blurted out the exhale of energy from pent up anxiety and it rushed through me like a bullet that had been fired.
The man stared at me. Said nothing. He thinks I'm crazy. Okay. I don't like this man. He's too selfish and way too arrogant for his own good. Okay. For You, God, I'll do this, because I love You so much. I folded my hands on the table top. I put my feet together on the floor. Sat up straight. Held my head high. Spoke with dignity.

"God says to tell you," I watched his face for some sparkle of acceptance to this holy introduction. Nothing. Blank. No expression.

Okay. Just do it. Obey God. "to tell you that He said He is hearing your prayers and not to do the thing you are planning to do today."

As I said this message the man started to tear up. I watched very large drops of water exit the man's eyes and splosh upon his starched white dress shirt. After what seemed like an eternity to me he slowly reached one hand out and hesitantly touched the top hand of my two hands folded on the table.

"Who are you?" His voice was a whisper of awe, like I might not be real and he had to check to see if I had real skin and bones on me.

I gained courage.

"That does not matter. Only God's message matters. He thought enough of you to take me out of two restaurants and drive me around town looking for you to deliver this message to you. So, I think it's important. Apparently it means something to you?"

He said nothing.

Fourteen Luke Five Six popped into my head. I wished I had my Bible with me to look that up, but I would have to look up Luke 14:5-6 later.

God, why did You make me run all over town to find this creep? He's so rude!

He slid his hand back to himself. Silent tears began running down his cheeks.

"I'm a pastor of a very large church here in town. I've sinned. I've sinned so bad there's no way out. I was driving home to commit suicide. I've been planning this for weeks. My wife isn't home now. I was going to lock myself in our garage and kill myself. I really was. Funny thing is I was just driving by this place when I got the strongest urge to come in. I don't know why here. I was just sitting here praying. You know. I know I'm going straight to hell for committing suicide but I deserve it. I told God I'm at the end of my rope. I'm going to kill myself today. My congregation will never forgive me. I've been stealing money from the church and someone found out about it. My wife will leave me when she finds out. I've been cheating on her. My life is over anyway."

Filthy dreadful victim leaver in the wake of your terrible sinful selfish horrid tormenting life. I thought. You hurt people to fill up your personal greedy selfish horrible creepy nasty self and don't even think about the pain you leave behind. I thought.

"Well. God says to tell you He is hearing your prayers and not to do the thing you are planning to do today," I said. "He must love you very much. He gave His life for you that you may have life. Your life has meaning and purpose. No problem is too hard for Jesus to fix."

"Yeah. Yeah. I've been preaching that for years."

I thought of how his wife would feel walking in on him in their garage. Finding him dead. Leaving her with great stigmas and soul searching as to why? What could she have done different? I started to judge the man as a real jerk and a coward to do that to everyone he would leave behind. I was feeling no mercy and my own victimization problems began to surface in my healing self and mind. I started to tell him that he would hurt his wife a lot. That corrective message would probably be followed by some more words of reprimand, but before I could say anything out loud God clearly spoke inside my spirit.

Get up and go now. Right now.

What God! Get up and go? But I just ... can't I ?

Right now.

Oh, okay, Lord. I was adding my own message to Your message, wasn't I. You don't want my human shame on him or my human judgment on him while You're redeeming him. I see. Forgive me Lord. I don't know how to love like You do. I don't know how to forgive like You do. I don't know how to not be harshly judgmental of people who really hurt other people. I hate people who leave victims strewn in their wake because they are selfish self centered cowards. He's a pastor! What a hypocrite.

I hate sin, too. Thank you, Sharon, for hearing and obeying me.

Holy Spirit, thank You. I know You are going to be talking to the man now. Thank You, Lord.

"John, we've gotta go now. Right now." I looked at my plate of uneaten food.
"Now?" John was starting on his second plate of all you can eat liver and gizzards.
"Yes."
"Okay."

I told John the story as I looked at myself in the visor mirror of our car driving home. "What in the world must that man have thought was talking to him?"
The visor mirror revealed my blonde wig had tilted and twisted askew from the sweat on my bald head. I had no eyebrows. My face was ashen grey. Chemo takes so much out of a person.
Here I was fighting so hard for my life and God sent me to a person who was going to take his life and snuff it out like a candle into darkness – like the gift of life meant nothing and was not worth fighting for.

I started to cry from experiencing the beauty and the unexplainable complexity of God's merciful compassion.
John reached his hand over and tenderly patted my arm.
"He just thought God sent him an angel to come save his life."

~~~~~~~~

Luke 14:5-6 *5. "Then he (Jesus) asked them, "If one of you has a son or an ox that falls into a well on the Sabbath day, will you not immediately pull him out?" 6. And they had nothing to say."*

WISDOM OF CHILDREN

Year: 1994

"Mom, don't you think you should start going to church?" The son who had snapped my picture on the pier when I saw the White Falconer in Galveston started to think it odd to have a Mom who claimed to talk with God and who would not go to church. I thought everybody knew I had claustrophobia and that I did not go to church because it would be rude to get up and leave in the middle of a sermon with a massive claustrophobic panic attack. My 'flee and flight' would take wing and rush me out to the nearest bathroom to hide with my fears and shame.

"Well ... "

I knew that my son had started going with a high school friend to a Bible teaching church in our home town. It is with great regret that I have to admit I never took either of my children to any church while they grew up. Husband nor children. None of us ever went to church or knew God.

I had for the past many months been cloistered alone in a room with Melodee's gift to me, a King James Version of the Bible, and a green hard backed dictionary, and an ever growing pile of my written study notes from God. The bindings completely wore off the Bible and dictionary from my daily use and investigation. God talked to me in my house. I studied in my house.

But ... maybe my son was right.

We started going to church. I got prayers. I got Bible studies. I got people and socialization. I got God therapy for my phobias. I went to the very first baby shower I had ever attended in my life. I went to church suppers. I went to a Christmas pageant.

I got lake baptized August 31, 1997. I got the Holy Ghost deeper and more wonderfully than ever before. I got learning. It was good.

During this time God sent me on many prophetic missions. I heard God. He taught me to hear my Master's Voice. I obeyed. I grew. God worked on my rotten character. God shoveled up and out the roots of my sins. The more work He did in me the more I realized there was a great amount that still needed doing.

I wrote down all the amazing messages from God. I studied the mysterious divine coded messages. I understood some and not others. I read them over and over. I grew some more. **I waited on the times maturing and the promises of God.**

MELODEE

I was standing at my kitchen counter with a piece of blank paper and a pen in my hand to start a shopping list. In the very moment that I thought I was going to begin by writing 'milk' ... God stopped my normal world and interjected His teachings, and these were to go on for a long and tremendously amazing time in my life.

Jesus moved the pen. I didn't move it. It was like that stick that drew His own feet on the beach at Corpus Christi. It was a miracle to me.

Apparently God thinks this is okay with Him if that's what it takes to get an agoraphobic, claustrophobic, house bound woman to finally pay attention to the things He wants to say.

The pen moved all by itself. And my hand surrounding the pen was moved by Holy Spirit talking to me about the things God says to us all the time, if we listen to heaven's chimes and hear the ring that is heaven's resonance to earth's resonance. Hello?! I saw words take shape, and then an entire sentence, from the Spirit of God.

I will favor those who speak in words that are a melodee to me. And so in song we live on together.

I stared at these words, then began to cry heavily with an abundant dose of Holy Spirit treat. Yes, a treat. A candy coated wish upon a star make a dream come true tastes good to me, treat — a sweet covering of healing and understanding. And years of heartache was taken into the healing rooms of God's plan.

*I will favor those who speak in words that are a **melodee** to me. And so in song we live on together.*

I was taken up into the holy places.

Revelation made me flood with tears of ecstatic joy at the same time as sad poignant loss ... a mixture of lovely blessings inside this moment.

'Melodee' was the name of my girlfriend in High School who had given me my first Bible. Melodee encouraged me to follow Jesus but I never even opened that Bible she gave me. It traveled unopened through my journey of hell. All along the answer was sitting right there, given to me by a friend whose name was Melodee.

God took this memory and paid sweet honor and tribute to Melodee. My friend had long ago been taken up to the Lord after a battle with cancer. Her witness to God was her whole life. Her testimony is the life she lived, full of the Joy of knowing the Lord Jesus and intimately experiencing His love of her.

I was the one on the outside who was really dead. Now my friend Melodee was gone on to heaven. I had been so sad that I could never tell her that I finally opened her Bible and met Jesus.

Here, in this play on words, Jesus gave tribute to 'Melodee', the name of my friend who gave me my Bible. God had sent into my lost life my Melodee to point me towards His Melody of Christ's holy love.

God had sent me His Song of Life. Somehow, in this moment of revelation from God, He helped to heal me from the guilt and shame I felt from never opening Melodee's gift until many years after she had died.

I will favor those who speak in words that are a melodee to me. And so, in song, we live on together.

I had wandered 40 years in the wilderness — when all along — the way and the direction had been placed as a gift in my very hand — and I had never used it to find the Promised Land that always was so near.

~~~~~~~~~~

Psalm 34: 4-5 *"I sought the LORD, and he answered me; he delivered me from all my fears. Those who look to him are radiant; their faces are never covered with shame."*

SHARON

Date: September 9

Sharon, what is your name?

My name? Well, my name is Sharon.

What is the name of my church?

I ... don't know. Will You tell me, Lord?

*Read Song of Solomon, my Song of Songs.
Take time to understand chapter two, verse one.*

Okay, Jesus. Let me look that up.
Here it is:

"I am a rose of Sharon, a lily of the valley."

Jesus! It's my name in Your Bible!

I call you, Sharon. Father loves you, Sharon. The tenor of Holy Spirit tells you things on Godly ground. Kindness waters your name and person. I love you.
I think that you thought you were just a thorn among thorns, and yet the truth is you are my Beloved. I think you thought that you were

lost, and here you are, found in my Loving Arms, my Bride. I think you told others that you were unimportant, how funny a thing to say, now you see, don't you, that you are the most cherished and highly important thing I ever laid my Eyes upon. I see a woman that shines forth brilliance. I see the radiance that you are. I see your worth and I am indelibly and incomparably in love with you, my dear one.

Forgive me Jesus, my dearest Throne of Grace. I knew not that Your love covers me. I knew not the heights of Your stellar proclamations that are You to me. I knew not your Love. Jesus, now I see. I am undone with the magnificent splendor of Your holy Person. I can see who You Are and this revelation is stunning. You are the ruby red of wisdom, and the golden sunset of old age. You are the treasure that I always knew was there to find, and now I am found by You.

Rose, I call you, and a Rose by any other name is still my rose.

I am Your servant Father God, please address me as Your true servant. Amen.

<u>Father in Heaven:</u>
Holy child, my Name of Sharon, your countenance pleases even me, and therefore I call you Sharon, my sweet rose. Jesus loves you, and He will take you across the bridge to me. Follow this great awakening and see things I only show my Bride. Amen.

<u>Jesus:</u>
Excavations underway. Peace ~ a wonderful new day. I call you my rose. I call you. Come into Communion with me, your Christ. Amen.

Oh My God! I just got the revelation, Jesus! Oh thank You for sending Your Holy Spirit to talk to us all and reveal to us things of God. Wow!!! And Wow!
I understand! I represent the Church! My name of Sharon! You are speaking to the Church! I am the 'church', like little 'c' 'church' because I am Yours individually and we are communing

personally, but You are prophetically explaining to everyone that the rose of Sharon represents the Bride who thinks she is worthless and not worthy ... Oh God, I cry with repentance for the things I have done against You. I see. Lord, You allow me to see. All I can say is I see that I am the church and that the rose of Sharon is the Bride. I am too weak from revelation to say more. Amen.

Communions With Christ

SONG

Date: 1995

Golden Girl, *pay attention, a Song is coming to the Church.*

A song? Thank You, Lord. You are good. Deeply good.
Golden Girl? Lord, please explain what that is? Thank You, my dearest tone of health. Amen.

Jesus Christ the Risen Savior that I AM tells you, my church, a SONG is coming to your rotundas, to your tabernacles, to your theology, to your self. I am sure I have told you already that your self is your spirit.

You are the Golden Girl. Amen, Christ, Jesus, Amen.

God in heaven, come down and tell me this secret thing. I place my self inside of the mysteries, if You will come to get me, allow me to live there in Your care. Amen.

Do you want to learn?

Please teach me. Everything, God. Teach me Your mysteries, please. The deep mysteries that You are. Oh Lord, I am Your Sharon at Your feet. Amen.

~~~~~~~~~~

GOD'S REVELATIONS

Jesus spoke into my days and spoke into my heart. His tumultuous training sessions included long lengthy hours upon hours of my recording the most amazing yet simple — and holy yet instructional teachings.

I was in the presence of God daily. I was whittled and pared upon like a willow tree, and the switch sometimes stung from God's reprimands. Yet the branch that I was being grafted into took my heart and transformed my incredibly ignorant thinking into a somewhat more lively and awake vessel. I sat up from my coffin and heard the Lord say to me, "Get up you dead dry bones, get up!"

His daily instructions usually consisted of me sitting down with a cup of tea in the morning, blank paper, Bible next to me, and a willing hand with a pen filled with enough ink to not run out that day, should the Lord decide to speak hours at a time, which He sometimes did!

I was softened, and taught by the Master Teacher.

I provide you with some of these things and hope that you will listen to the Lord talk to you, as He will be telling you your own lessons and these will apply to your own personal journey.

~~~~~~~~~

Communions With Christ

INDEPENDENCE

Date: July 4, 1995

*C**hrist Jesus:*

Freedom is a precious thing.
Its fight is won by heroes
Who recognize that
In a Victory over oppression
There is true Independence.

~~~~~~~~~~

I CANCEL OUT THE PLACE

Date: July 5, 1995

I CANCEL OUT THE PLACE

Uh. What Lord!

WOMAN JETS AND EMERGE GAMMA RAYS

Excuse me?? Woman jets and emerge gamma rays?

I call you by the name of Woman, my church. You Jet. You Emerge Gamma Rays. It is so. It will be done. And Amen.

What??? What place do you cancel out?

I cancel out the place of ignorance and rotten fermenting horror. And from inside the woman shall emerge forth from obscurity the electromagnetic radioactive gamma rayic decay and fall out that has been plaguing the earth's surface decade upon decade, and rise to be no longer immersed within hate, corruptness, greed, and terrorization. And God in Heavenly Grace shall kiss your tender outstretched arms and then, oh woman, my holy one, wedded with my love, you shall fly as a rose bud opening and this trail shall beautify the skies with gamma rays transmitting joy to all, heavens included.

THE ONE SON SHALL ACHIEVE GREATNESS

God, I don't know what this means.

The lesson is a metaphor. I will teach it.
I, Jesus, am saying these words to you.

PENCILS

Date: August 30, 1995 — 11:00AM

*P**lease record the chapter on PENCILS.*

Yes, Lord. I hear Your Voice and I will write it all down. Thank You.

Okay, here we go students. Please pick up your pencils. You will need them to write with, in Spirit School. Blessed is the pencil. It allows thoughts to be written down. My Ways are fun to learn. Yes?
Come sit at my feet and let me teach you, sweet children of mine. In the Reason is an Intellect. The name of Reason is Logos, or, Eternal Being showing you what is. Each student should learn that the Logos is inseparable from the Word of God, which is Jesus Christ.
So, if in a test I was to say to you, "Student, what is inseparable from the Word Jesus Christ?" — you would answer with your pencil, "Logos". That is good! Student you make an 'A' on your first test. See? I told you I was a Fun Teacher.
My name is Fun. I AM your Teacher. I Am Jesus Christ, in Whom all Life is given to you by our Father God by grace.
Jesus Christ as Savior is where you wish to reside. So, student, learn about the Truth. And Amen.

Now. Second lesson.

What is the name of your Teacher who is Jesus Christ?

The student who did pay attention in class would write with his pencil, "Your name is Fun. And your name is Jesus Christ is Life. Your name is Truth and Savior!"

And then, because you know me by the name of Fun, and by the name of Life, and also because you know me to be telling you Truth, you would again make an 'A' on your test score. Behold! A star student in the making. My precious child whom I love in great and tender care, good job!

It is my Father in Heaven who gives to me the lessons that I teach to you. For I and my Father are One. We are Fun. Also I tell you that all you need to know will call you blessed and will take you greatly within to find that Temple Place to secret doors and fortune untold, yet the treasure is there to give away. You receive this treasure the moment that you hear this Godly gift, the Voice, as it is by the Voice that holy help councils within you. This Voice is Holy Spirit's tenor.

Now. Lesson Three. What is my Father's Name?

The students who write with their pencils: "The Word God In Heaven Is Your Father, and you speak by way of Him, my Jesus Fun Life." — those, including all, receive another 'A', of which you now have, according to my report card, a Triple A average. What a brainiac you are!

Receive a Triple Star Award!

Recess now. You may go out to play in the yard, students. But please notice all the equipment in Yeshuah's school yard. All equipment is Fun in the Name of the Lord. None other.

If you stumble over anything else — you are in the wrong school yard. And run like crazy back to Jesus Fun Life School House to play in recess amongst what the Teacher has provided for you to amuse you while you are waiting for the **Bell to chime.**

It is good that my lessons have retained themselves in you while you go out to play. I tell you to stay within the hearing of my **Bell**.

You can hear my school house bell calling you back to me to sit and absorb yet another lesson still.
There. The bell chimed. Time to return for another fine lesson from your Teacher whose name is Fun. I told you we would begin with two plus two.

Excuse me, Jesus. I don't recall You telling me we would begin with two plus two. Did I miss something?

Oh Jewel with the hand raised up to me in perpetual curiosity, we sit and speak so well because you listen, and you absorb, and you question. And you want to know my inner heart.
And so, class, I shall take time to answer Sharon's question. I did tell you all we would begin with two plus two when I created you. I have within your DNA a coded trail of development, the perpetual evolution that spiritually we must travel on. I wake you, in Seal One. I make you in Seal Two. I create you in Seal Three. I orchestrate you in Seal Four. I ovate you in Seal Five, and I stimulate you in Seal Six. I speak of the dimensional bending that takes place within holiness. I will tell you these things in another lesson, class. I, learned Teacher, know what you are able to take, and a milk drink for today is sufficient. And Amen.

Now. I continue with the lesson. Two plus two. Basics of laws that are unalterable. Two plus two is Four. Three and One is Four. Four is the dimension that you wish to build yourself into. I will take you there if you will follow me.
*My dear students, it is the man who takes into his eternal form the Name of Jesus Christ which is Fun In The Lord's Life Is Saved who sees the **BELL'S** New Lights.*
And so, you may ask, what this Bell is? I leave this up to you to engage upon a journey of discovery. I am the Buoy and I come ashore to teach you that I am coming. Great that thou art, oh woman, holy wife and bride, the tank is filling up, my love it over flows.
*New Lights are the heaven's filaments. Beauty lies within. The lesson for you to ponder on, to memorize, and to be able to recall with **experiential** accuracy to anyone who should ask you the*

question: "What goes on in that School House?" — *you can take your pencils and write across the skies of time "The Teacher of Life talks to us about Love and Life, and I seem to be getting healthier while I listen to Him!"*

Really? They will ask. "Can I get into that School House?" And this is when you will recall your lesson, and what you have memorized in your heart. This is when you write into the hearts of those who ask you how to enter into the School House: "The man who takes to his eternal form the Name of Jesus Christ, which is Fun in the Lord's Life, is saved. And he shall enter into learning by the Teacher of Truth."

Then if your friend asks you what that means, say that All Is Eternal. But some places are not so fun to be in, in an eternal state. In my Teacher's Classroom inside the Temple walls of Life building, **Gated** *thresholds shall appear to the man who takes my hand. And Father will lead my holy children by His Spirit to the Throne rooms, secret treasured places, within Holy Majesty, yours inside of this Kingdom of God that lies within His Heart. And Amen.*

Recess again.
Gee.
Isn't fun school nice? No long boring lectures. Just fun. I who in formal times was called Jesus am the Heart of Fun pumping out My Blood to all students with pencils in their willing hands to learn from me. Amen.

I call you my rose of Sharon. I call you my Bride, my love, my darling. Record me in the earth. Kindly take the lesson to be learned and, for your children, leave it here to know when their children come. They, your grandchildren, can have the heart of the Father, too.

Receive your thank you, my rose of Sharon, my church unto my will being done in earth as it is in heaven. You are my dearest worker in the Garden of Love. Amen.

~~~~~~~~~

Communions With Christ

THE ERASER

Date: August 30, 1995 – 12:00 Noon

*W*e shall now write the chapter called *THE ERASER*.

Okay, Jesus! I am looking forward to what You say in Spirit School to me. This is so fun! Amen. I just hold the pen and You move my hand! Incredible! I never know what the next word will be. Your Holy Spirit tells me the Truth. I know Your Voice. I am so excited to hear what You will teach next! You are the most amazing and fascinating Person. I love being in love with the Maker of my salvation. Amen.

School contains many fun things.
Pencils *to write down the WORD of God.* **The Window That Brings In More Light. Song.** *Time in* **Choir practice**, *where the Teacher is a real neat Guy who has a perfect ear for beautiful sounding music. And, of course,* **Lunch Time**, *where we get to eat good foods that make us healthy.*
School has many good things. But one **'in particular'** *is very important to the Teacher. It is* **THE ERASER**.
Pay attention class, says the Fun Teacher, who is Jesus the Christ of your salvation.

I Am the Teacher. This is My Eraser.
I Am the One who erases the blackboard.

Ha ha ha ha ha.
All class stares at Fun Teacher who makes a funny joke.
The student who has read his homework assignment will know that he has gained a Spiritual Councilor to Guide him in things at school. The student who has studied his lessons that his Holy Spirit Guide told him to read before starting school today will understand why we need to erase the 'black' of the slate I write upon. I teach you Truth.
Clue: In the black of the slate board is a heart of STONE and black is the error of its form.

So. In my classroom is The Eraser.
We can see that The Eraser is full of chalky white chalk while it erases the black board after each lesson. Students, see that the writing on the black board is White and that The Eraser is picking up all of the particles of the flowing words that are now within The Eraser which is rubbing itself against the black of the slate of stone.
The Eraser takes the White words and fills itself up with Love.

*I particularly like the **particle**. It picks up so much knowledge.*
*The Fun Teacher always writes across the black board in White letters of Knowledge. Jesus, who is your Teacher, now says to my students fair, **"The Fun Teacher In Whom I AM Always Writes Across The Black Board In White Letters Of Knowledge."***
Scholarly students who study symbolism can please interpret for the classroom.

Is there a meaning that You can tell us now, Jesus?

Class? Do I have a hand raised from my students? Is there an interpreter of symbolism in this classroom? From the front row rises a hand of a student. Jesus calls upon the hand risen to Him.
The Front Row Hand states, "Jesus, my Teacher, do You mean that the black of satan is written over by the White Light Of God's Wisdoms when You write upon the black boards of our schools? Do You cover over the darkness with Your White Light and Your Word

when You write with the Word of God that so needs to be taught to the students of Your School?"

Jesus, who teaches in a fun way, replies, "Student whose hand is raised up to me, I acknowledge your knowing. And I reward you for being in my room. Amen."

Recess again.
Gee. *School is fun.*
Play upon the pencils the drumbeat of a Note of God.
Play upon the Sway of the Swing.
Play upon the Eternal Opus in the Key of G.
Read the signs in the play yard. They all are the Holy Spirit's Voice ~ Guide's posted notes upon the frontlets of His Robe.
Bells *of Reason call.*
School is in session yet again.

While the class was at recess the Fun Teacher, who is God in Jesus Name, has been cleaning His erasers. He has been banging all the white chalk out of The Eraser to make room for more to accumulate in The Eraser as it passes over the black board that needs to be erased.

Where goes the chalk falling from The Eraser? Into the air of the School Room. Into the noses and lungs of the students who come to learn of God. The room is filled with the dust of the white chalks of the lessons which have been written upon the black board with the White Word of God.

With a broad stoke of His holy hand the erasers bang together. And Voila! Dust.
Particles of White about the room. Remains of the life that was in the words that Class was taught. Letters of Knowledge remaining.
The particles remain. *Even if they are not seen as words, the dust and the residue of the White Word of God, which is written in the heart of each student by the Teacher Jesus Christ across the black board of stone, of slate, these white words of His teachings remain in the students who saw it, read it, knew what it meant.*

These white words of His teachings remain in the air for all the students of the Word to breath in and to ingest, as particles of wisdom which are carried on the wings of the Holy Ghost ~ and Guided into the precious beings who are students of the Truth.

Holy.
Holy is the way of God.
And the person in the Front Row with his hand raised to God knew inside of him what it all meant.
"I am a child of God," said the student to Jesus Christ. "And You, my Teacher, stand before me at the black board of my life, trying with all of Your Might to fill up my day with Your great Self. Even when I go out to play, You remain vigilant in attendance to my preparation. You wipe away the blankness of my mind – a mind filled with empty silly error – and You write upon my mind a Spirit filled life to live."

"You give me the chance to see the Word of Your life, and to live in this Word forever. And all of the dust of the Word which You sacrificed at Calvary does float into my self, a student at Your feet in learning."

"Oh my Teacher, I adore You.
The School of Revelation is so sweet. Blessed is the School of Revelation in the Holy Spirit. Blessed art Thou, oh my Teacher, whose Name above all names is Jesus Christ, the Eternal Risen God."

I am speechless, Lord!

I just sit here with pieces of blank paper and a pen in my hand and You move my hand! You write Your mind for me to know You! I don't think of any of these words, Father God. Your Holy Spirit tells me what to write and it takes shape on the page as spiritually discerned and given words without my ever thinking at all of any of these words. You are talking God. I am supremely grateful. And Father, this gift from You is surely Divine. Thank You.

I am receiving Your Spiritual giftings. You are telling me the Mind that You are. I think You are amazing.

Why are You making my hand move automatically to write these things from Your mind to me? These pages of writing look so strange. It's just the train of thoughts from You with no stops to dot the i's or cross the t's or spaces between the words. Thank You, God.

Read Romans 8:6.

Oh! Okay, God. Let me look that up!

Romans 8:6 ***"The mind of sinful man is death, but the mind controlled by the Spirit is life and peace."***

Jesus, who stands upon the floorboards of the School House, guides a smile into the student's heart ~ For understanding is grand. It is how the Teacher who is fun intends to teach His class. Amen.

~~~~~~~~~~

Communions With Christ

LUNCH TIME

Date: August 31, 1995

*L*unch time, class.
Please be sure you eat healthy foods when you make your selection at the cafeteria of the Fun School House.
  <u>Peaches.</u> Pleasant words within your self speaking out to others.
  <u>Plums.</u> Outward appreciation of the help you get from others.
  <u>Perfume.</u> Incense to my nose. <u>Kindness given out of your heart to another heart so special to me.</u>
  <u>Persuasion.</u> Getting the best place you can in the line that I give you to be invested within in your life time as a man. This means, be a superb being at what ever you endeavor to do. Eat of this pleasure, the pleasure of doing your sweet best for me.
  <u>Pancakes.</u> <u>Manna.</u> <u>Given every day unto you.</u> Eat it up, for it lasts only for a day, and dries up tomorrow.
  <u>Purple.</u> Invest in the wisdoms of my Church. And believe in me.

  Now go back to the classroom for another lesson. Full and fat with pleasantries you have eaten at the snackery of life. In sanctuary I AM Jesus and Amen.

  Lord, thank You for this lesson. I wish that I would remember this always. But the words are so, so deep, Father. I know I will have to read and study these and more of your Word to understand the full banquet You lay before us daily. I love You, Lord. Amen.

~~~~~~~~~~

CHOIR PRACTICE

Date: September 5, 1995

*O*h *students in my classroom, slip in behind your chairs. Stand upon the floorboards of wood. Ready yourselves to sing. I am your Fun Teacher and I shall be in attendance for this Choir Practice.*

I tap my baton upon the lectern. I study my notes. I look into the eyes of each student, to see the potential for song's reverie.

I call you all by name.
For What Is In A Name?

*Oh **Johnny** boy, you look so round with holy tone. The Lord is your salvation. Your God is Jehovah. Grace unto you now.*

*Oh **Shannandoah**, you come all singing across the meadows to school today. The hills are alive with your song. Sing on. I open up your flow, my Shannandoah. In all the river of your flow, find your path to me. Practice. Be beautiful. Join a sea that floods the heights. I ask you, can you swim? The flow takes you on. Be wise my love. Flow to me. My river of life is Shannandoah's lips kissing my shores in stellar heights.*

Okay now.

*Oh **Joshua**, you liken to a roe, a deer, calm, and slim, svelte and perky with an emittance that sounds like a roe cutting across a forest* *of trees in foliage. Joshua, in all of your being you are aware that I AM what I AM. Victory to you.*

Oh **Jezebel**, *your voice is cranky, not full of grace, not grand with passion. I think you sound like murky mud within my choir. Please shut up. The unbridled passion of your sense consciousness is unproductive.*

Oh **James**, *I supplant your voice with notes that take you into an illuminated choir. I give your lesson special care. For James, you travel into me. In shores above the stellar sea, we blend in harmony.*

Oh **Harold**, *I call to thee, and you do answer with a tone which pleasantly rises up to the ears of angels with a perfect pitch. My champion, you supply the battlefield with holy love, and you take my strength into the battle with you. I bless you for eternity. And Amen.*

Oh **Bonnie**, *you skip across the fields with your wheat-like golden throat, singing all the others into their place of joy. I ask you maiden fair to marry me. Today. Do not delay, my Bride, come home.*

Oh **Sally**, *you are new here. You do not know the song. But you want to. Listen. Learn it. The Song of the Master Teacher. Sally, venture forth. Issue from your besieged position an attack upon the enemy.*

I tap upon the podium and we all begin.

Harold *sings out loudest, reverberating his strong song to me. Echoing across the valleys and pulling them up to hill tops.*

Lincoln, *you cheerfully round your notes to sing like they should be. You are my breed of sheep. And your long wool shall cover thee.*

And **Sarah**, *you make a sound that takes my heart away to bliss. Noble woman ~ my daughter of the King. Your song should never be allowed in any way to unite with matter or material conditions.*

Favor upon you, my Choir practice. You make me smile as you sing in the school house of the Fun Teacher. Amen.

Oh Teacher, Christ, Lord, Father, Holy Spirit, The One! It seems like You have just told me the names of the persons we have inside of us, the church, and the Church, the Body of Christ, that can practice and sing the song Truth is. Love. I think You are teaching me the way to Love You and to be in the Tune You are.

I see the journey, Father. It is the journey that You send each of us on who apply our self to learning the music that the heavenly place is. I am undone. Just raptured with this revelation. I see so much, yet I see nothing. I know at the same time that I do not know. I can only thank You, Jesus, for talking to me this way.

I know that You are talking to all of us, every human being here in this place we call earth. The fact is, Lord, we are the Body of You Christ, right? While here in this earthly place? And we must function in unison and in harmony to be the Melody that You say lives on forever to Your ring tone. Amen?

That is very insightful of you, Sharon. This training thing is very fun and yet the journey takes every person through many levels of transformation. I love each of the ones who call me King. Many names are the names within the Body of Christ, my Church.

I call you each "my choir" and apply the same principles to each student. The goal is to sing in harmony with the One who Teaches you my Melody.

I give you the scales, you practice for awhile, and you come to class again, singing better, and get the next line of musical arrangement to learn. I train the voice to hear the Voice. In each student that comes to class I give a DNA chain of alterable sequential reverberation, and so, lift up your eyes and sing to me my Song. And Amen.

Thank You for being in charge of Choir Practice, Lord. Amen.

I have given you a list of names. Much is in a name. Much is in my Body of Christ as my Woman flies away to glory with me.
Read First Corinthians 12: 12-15.

Yes, Lord. I will read that immediately!

1ˢᵗ Corinthians 12: 12-15 "12. *The body is a unit, though it is made up of many parts; and though all its parts are many, they form one body. So it is with Christ. 13. For we were all baptized*

by one Spirit into one body — whether Jews or Greeks, slave or free — and we were all given the one Spirit to drink. 13. Now the body is not made up of one part but of many. If the foot should say, "Because I am not a hand, I do not belong to the body," it would not for that reason cease to be part of the body."

Particles. Filaments. *Take these and supply them with my Name.*

I am **Concave Residue** *supplying the earth with the Glory Tune. I come into the earth and concave the song to teach you with the reverberations from my next Dimension.*

I leave behind your inheritance, my will, and the remains of this will for you are unalterable, and incontestable. In this residue, you will inherit the estate if you come forth and claim your rightful place as my child. And Amen.

Inhibitors. *I send angels to inhibit the flow of rot towards heaven and supply the life to you that is actuated in the angelic mission.*

Ovational Bliss. *The wisdom of Glory is Ovational and the Bliss it brings to you is Glorious. It is a place to travel within. I give The Bliss Tune to my Earth inside of the human beings who hear the Tune I sing to you, my own dear students.*

The feet of the Teacher tells you the tune.

I am in love ~ the tune that my love plays that you can hear ~ the tune you need to hear ~ the tune I play so rapturiously to you is **JOY.** *I am buried in Joy.* **I rise up and call you to be risen with my JOY.** *Amen and Christ the risen Lord speaks to you. Amen.*

I love my Choir. Notes of Beauty to my ears.

But the silly decibels of gong will be eliminated from my musical array.

~~~~~~~~~

Communions With Christ

SING ALONG

Date: September 7, 1995

*G*olden Girl, **Golden girl**, *pay attention, sing along, trill the notes, fill the cavities of emptiness, and rejoice, a Song is coming to the Church.*

The Song?? Thank You, Lord. How do I sing this Song?

You are learning. Good work. Keep listening to the sounds of the heartbeat I sent to you and now you finally hear.

This is for my whole Church, Sharon. I am the Bridegroom and I come to speak to my Bride. Your mission, dear daughter, is to write down the things I tell you. You are my Scribe, Seer, Sharon. I thank you for this jolly reverent time we have with each other. I love you, too, Sharon.

Do unto me as You will, and through Your power and might, Amen.

Now class, I answer your questions. Any questions?
__Harold?__ Yes? What do you want to know?
I hear you ask me, Harold, **"What is the mighty noise out of the windows of the classroom? The roar of the wind? Is the noise the siphoning off of a mighty hurricane's pull upon the land?"**

No, Harold, I shall tell you, my victorious lad. I love you Harold, and the sound you hear is **my own Song**.
And so we shall learn about my SONG.
Pencils ready? Record for me, my class.
I am a recording device.
Your life is 'in' the recording of my device. You are within the recording of my sound chamber, pencils writing the score of your own tune to me.
I alter the pitch. I ambulate the sway.
I concave the trill. I eliminate the gong.
I sustain you in my SONG's pitch. I love you.

Your ambulatory, concaved whistle is the supply of your sound cavity. The sound cavity that you are, within God's plan to be all that you can be, this sound filtering devise ... before you go on pray ...

Lord, I thank You for this revelation and I ask You, Jesus, to give me the words — not me give me the words, Amen.

God's devise is the plan by the will of the Maker of your spirit to take you into the inherited days that you are going to be inheriting, and this is real property and real value and real purpose, and it is the sound filtering devise that tells you with clarity your purpose as spirit, and this has within the devise a fulcrum effect that takes you into the Great beyond of space ~ into the holy places ~ and this watershed life you live is given tunes, and this water of life, and tributary of water's flow ... spiritual life water's flow, these and more are what is within your body of flesh, as a 'third note' being.
I am the Lord God telling you that a 'third note' being is the person who lives the journey within the 'third dimension of earth's resound'.

I have many sheep pens and they all need my attention for theirs is a song which is part and particle of the Whole Note.

In the earth is your resound. **In the third dimension of your self is your third Octave being gravitationally readied to pull up,** *or out, of the Opus. In my Opus in C Major, pun meaning that the Christ takes the Major, ha ha, (you will understand this one day, Sharon), in this Opus of my numbered sequential overtures within your spiritual long flow, your talent takes the initiative and plays your recital for me. It is your resound.*

You resound to me, and you become within the recording, within the yardstick of beautiful measure. The 'measure' is a musical term in this case, class.

The song you hear, Harold, outside of the windows of the class room, *(outside the classroom that The Triple Time tells you of the Song He Is),* **it is simply the dimensions calling you to come into their classroom to see and to know about my higher Spirit. Amen and Amen.**

Harold, *body of my juxtaposed lines upon a graft that is a* **measure of joy to me, see in the chart the number 'seven'.** *It is a lined chart, a measure that contains seven.* **I lift up the score, and I make more music in each measure of the invisible line which is within my life to know.**

Lord, did You say 'graft'? Is Harold "upon a graft"? I hear Your Spirit's Voice phonetically while You are writing all these words, and You wrote 'graft'. I was wondering if You mean 'Harold is upon a 'graph'?

I graft the Choir into my Body, Sharon. I say that Harold is the Tenor of the Choir and His Victory March heralds the Won Day. Amen.

Oh Jesus. You graft us in to You! I see all that is holy is grafted within holiness together inside the Body of Christ the graft tells the juxtaposed lines which time in musical measure to play ... I ... Oh ... Lord, I can't see any more. Will You please continue in this lesson? Thank You, Amen.

It is with great pleasure that I convey to your minds the will of mine. The will of mine that you inherit, this inheritance of my will, is contained within a SONG.

Here is my SONG.
I am the Resonant Pitch.
I escalate the reverberation.
I take you Home. Withstanding the sway of the downward pull, the song's 'jib' becomes 'consonance'. A ship of life this jib sails by, a triangle of Three, all sides the same, and One Sail this jib, One. Golden sunsets and tribulational waters sail mesmerizingly through the days of life on earth, and they, the ones who hear the song, they are the ones I give my home to. I call your song upward and you fly into my pitch. I elevate the dissonance into the trill. I invert your 'self', and polarity changes you into the Fourth dimension.
I tell you — and so remember that I tell you — 'self' is your spiritual journey — all the way of it is your 'self'.
Remember that I tell you this — your 'self' is spirit.
In this Fourth dimension your song does sound so sweet to me. I lift your sweet song into the Dell. And we do play the Rose's Parade of Glory to each other. Amen.

I see the truth, God.
I see the dimensions that You speak of, traveling throughout the mansions of Your Home, bringing history to Your gown and holiness to Your throne, and my self to Your arms in love. Holy Father, life is in this place. Amen.

I give you eyes to see, my holy Sharon. What is in a name?
I tell you class that in my Seven Seals I ambulate the waltz, and also the 4/4 time, and I do with this melody that which I need to 'trill', so as to trade out 'what was' for what 'takes its place' in your 'self' — and ... What is 'self' class? All together now ~ 'My self is my spirit, Teacher!'
Good students!
Gee!
Always Gee!
I can cancel out the place that was and I gather the winds and fire your spirits up to the Fifth Seal.
I am the Melody. I will tell you about Melody.
I call you the Melody of Life.

In the 'tone' you are 'singularly you'. One note is the spirit that you are, no other spirit takes this note to his life to play. However, in this single tune you may alter the pitch. I actually alter your pitch. I alter your resonant transitory spiritual life through the door and we fly into the Fourth Seal.

I then ambulate the whole rhythm band and play to you in 4/4 time. I make a little musical pun. I am allowed to be fun and to have fun because I am the 'conductor'. Ha ha!

I am the Conductor of this Orchestration, and I conduct the electrical Latitudes and transitory overlays that tabulate the beings you are.

Fun School and Fun Life are the Trajectory of Joy's own students.

Now then class, joyfully know that this 'melody', 'trill', and 'grand opus in construction', then craves to be played with more gusto, and so, particles of resound fill the echo chambers that are Sealed in the other dimensions and take you onward.

I am in succession taking your grand spiritual song through the Seven Seals. I speak of the resolute Third Seal, the Fun Fourth Seal, the Fifth Seal which is regulatory again, the Sixth Seal that is only my dearest trill, and the Seventh Seal, and your holy note is complete. Amen.

I tell you of my Melody. Hear this sound, and follow this, for you are in the journey that leads to life in the whole Note. Amen.

Holy Father, I wish to offer You my prayer of repentance for saying any words or allowing anything into my life that would disrespect You or the life You are trying to create in Love. I concede that the wonders of eternal fire are found in You as You fashion me. Forgive me for uttering any words that are profane to the holy image of Christ. Remove stain from me. Remove the errant heart from me. Come to me in mercy, Holy Father God, and help me to recognize the notes that hold the keys to the music to Your ears. Amen.

~~~~~~~

Communions With Christ

PLOWING FIELDS

Date: September 17, 1995

Gee. I see a plow. Its forehead is a frontlet. In its pouch is sacraments of old. In the brow of the plower is all that Eternal speaks. Fortune enters. His name is Benjamin. In Ephesian Fields he gleans.

> *Sharon, I give you a wonderful inheritance.*
> *It is the gift of prophecy from my heart to your heart.*
> *Amen. Live it out. Amen.*
> *Read Proverbs 9:6.*

Yes, Lord. I'll look that up now.

Proverbs 9: 6 *"Leave your simple ways and you will live; walk in the way of understanding."*

Inside of the pouch are nuggets. Golden are the stones. Invested filaments of Gold. Given unto you. Place them in your brow and eat of the foods I send you.

Bended with the sun from daybreak to sundown ~ the Farmer grows his crops. Every way that is inside the sun's day is grown in fields that ripen quick.
Wholeness ~ purposed unto its day ~ comes placidly into yield.

Word God, in Whom I Am, is going to give to you, student whose hand is raised to me in my never ending classroom ~ the formula for success.

I give to you my prophecy. In white the legacy of the Falconer is the winged birds in flight. The earth can change her battery by Wonder over-night. The sun can spin. The veil can fly. The Bride can look upon me. Begin, oh day in wedding processional. Widen, Eternal Holy Spirit, the place I call my decision. Oh room in Third dimensional bending, widen for the increase that is coming into thee. Oh plane, widen in me.

I divide my wheat from my chaff.
In my plowing fields is workmanship done, and my plowing fields are bursting with ripened fruits.
Holy blessings I send to you, oh my wonderful holy church. In my Name receive the blessings upon my Name Jesus in Love. Joy. Amen.

Yes, Lord. Thank You Jesus for baptizing me in Your Holy Spirit. Thank You for Your gifts. Amen.

Prophetic word is your gift. Home is your Direction. Star of Wonder is your Guide. White is your halo. Wedded is your state in wonder within Jesus Holy God.

~~~~~~~~~

Communions With Christ

GEE

Jesus, I was just wondering, why do You say 'Gee'? It sort of sounds funny to have God talk like You do. I mean You say, "Gee, it's lunch time." Or, "Gee, I see a plow." Or, "Gee, it's recess time." Once You said, "Gee. Always **Gee**." Am I missing something?

Oh my lovely. You are so sweet.
Listen to the Word of the Lord. **'Gee' is a command to my people to hear my Voice and obey its direction.**
I say, "Gee. I see a plow."
I am talking in very syllogistic parables and very subjective and spiritual words that are extremely deep and symbolic when I talk to you, my dear.
"Gee. I see a plow." I am referring to the command **"GEE — Turn to the right my workers in the fields. I see a plow."**
'I see a plow' means 'I see you'. **You are the plow.** *I see a plow means I see your self (and what is your self?) tilling and toiling all the day long for me. I see you as the plow putting your heads down and rowing my fields to drop the seeds into grounds that have been made ready by your toiling. The seeds of my chosen crops go into the rows and these seeds fall upon the grounds. Soils differ, yet the plow always plants the seeds and hopes to see the seedling grow into the desired fruit. Yes?*
And remember, your self is your spirit. I see your self tilling and toiling all the long day long for me.

When a Farmer takes his oxen into the field he tells them which direction to go. If I was the Farmer and you were the oxen I would say, "Gee." And then, my flock, you, as my 'plowing ground devices', you would turn to the right.

The term "gee" means the command "Turn to the Right, my oxen pulling the plow of my commanding rows of corn and wheat" ~ and farmed land appears ~ abounding with holiness.

Kindly obey and "Gee" because I love you, my sheep.

I shear my sheep. I tend my cattle on a thousand hills.

I AM.

Oh my Lord. Just the majestic mystery of You astounds my simple soul. Please keep telling me the mystery of who You are. Amen, with gratitude.

See more, Sharon. You are my Seer, prophet. Enjoy the sights in heavenly chambers. I thank you for coming into the tabernacle and entering with my holiness to chat. This is a good thing you do, and we are in love, right?

Lovingly You send me these pictures in my spirit. Your Love is overwhelming. Spirit of revelation encompasses me now. I can see the Right as a color wheel spinning towards total White, the totality of knowing all that is Good and Love.

I see You, Father. You are in the grandest hall ~ a hall of openness ~ a wholeness divided up to give us each a home within Christ a place of Total. Total fullness. A place within that which is Right.

Right means many things, I see this now, Lord, from Your perspective, high up in the heavenly place where You sit in High Great Truth. I see Right to mean Greatness Achieved within our son of God that we birth by Your birthing into us the awareness that Christ talks and God is Christ.

Also I see Right meaning Gold. I see Right meaning Glory. I wish You would show us all how to Gee and turn to the Right. This is a great command and one we should fear not to heed from our Maker.

Please, Lord, seek us out and fill us with intense understanding of what You ask of us when You say "Gee". Thank You, Lord. Amen.

I am taking you into my chambers, seer. You are given sight, Sharon, because I choose you to see me. And never doubt that I have sought you out and I have chosen you. Amen.

I will still endeavor to have no doubt with Your holy help. It is when I place myself there in the **'being without doubt'** location that I seem to commune with You so freely. People tell me that I do not hear you, God. But I know we talk face to face, Lord. Amen.

I see your face and facing you is my holiness for you to see. Amen.

~~~~~~~~~~

Communions With Christ

TELL ME

It had been raining all night. A great and terrible storm. Lightening, thunder, oppression of barometric pressure that felt like my flesh was being crushed against my bones. I remember folding laundry in the den. John was on the couch reading his newspaper. The weather continued to drizzle outside, skies grey and gloomy. No where to go today but take this Saturday off and stay inside.

And then. I knew.

"John, I'm going to go out."

"But it's raining. Where?"

"I don't know. God is telling me to go out on another mission."

"Do you want me to go with you?" John was concerned for my safety.

"No, I think I have to do this one alone."

"Take your cell phone."

Within a few minutes I was in my car. I had no other compass than the Holy Spirit that talked within my spirit and told me things of Godly relevance. Things that astounded even me, continually. Never have I lost my awe and amazement for the things of God.

Traveling north, past open country side and cows in fields, twisting winding country back roads, and then I realized. My destination was a neighboring town called Denton. I have always thought this town charming in just certain spots, where old world charm meets eclectic University growth. There are many turn of the century homes, styles of architecture not built any longer, preserved, and some are now taken over by college students who call these home for a learning term.

I just metered out my driving, listening, thinking, hearing, analyzing, discerning, believing God was at the wheel. And I was just the one He sent out. Like one of the birds on the arm of this White Falconer who sends His birds inland to do His work and bring back a bird of prey where that bird will then sit upon the arm of God and be fixed. I had experienced it many times.

Oh. Okay, Lord. I see.

I got my commanding orders from my General in Chief. God said to stop at the church on the corner, get out of my car, and wait upon His further instructions. I was of course hearing all of this inside of my spirit, the spirit that God was talking to, and I just had given myself to the process of trying to learn how to hear and obey His will in my life.

I saw a lethargically wasted pile of dead bones covered by a young man waiting down the road. As soon as I stood on the corner of the intersection next to the Catholic Church this greatly threatening boy began to move towards me. He took purposed steps and stared right at me. I looked around to see if, (please God!), there was someone else standing behind me that this wretched young man was looking at. But nope. It was me. And me alone.

Standing on this rain soaked street corner in the gloomy lightless grey of the rainy day I was terror stricken.

He was a very dark person. I mean his spirit. Darkness shouted loudly off of him in great waves of ions screaming for help out of every cell of his body.

His dress was dismal. A dark black tee shirt with an ever approaching theme of words that told me he worshipped satan. His baggy pants and old shoes shuffled his slumped body right up into my face. His black hair was spiked upwards with grease or mousse or just a very bad night's sleep and a bad hair morning.

He was taller than me. He could flatten me.

God! NO! Please no! I can't take on a satan worshipper! NO Lord! No!

You are Strong.

God don't make me do this! Jesus! I'm begging you! God, I don't know what to do!

I am with you.

The teen's eyes met mine. His dark black eyes had red eyeliner drawn around them. Will he pull a knife and stab me and kill me on the spot? Mug me? Spit on me? Drop kick my carcass to the curb and wipe his shoes on me?

Fear not, satan is a speck of dust under your big toe.

A calm came over me. God quieted the storm inside my fearful heart.
"Are you the priest?"
"WHAT?"
"Are you the priest? I'm supposed to meet a priest here."
"Oh. You are?" Relieved, I looked around and read the name of the Catholic Church on the sign. Immaculate Conception. "Oh, well, then! Just go on into the church and there will probably be a priest inside!"
"God, thank You for letting me off the hook!"

You are the priest.

"I can't get in the church. I've already tried. The door's locked."
"What!" I was of course exclaiming disbelief at what God was telling me, not answering the satan worshipper's comment about the locked church door.
"I said the door's locked! Are you deaf? I'm supposed to meet a priest here. I've been waiting outside here in the rain all morning."
"You have? Well, what's the name of this priest?"
"Are you the priest?"
"Um. Uh."

You are the priest.

"Well ... um. Okay. Uh. You see ... um. If you ... uh. I ... that is ... um ... well ... "

I wrestled with God in my spirit. He gave me a choice. I wrestled for what seemed like a long time to me, and then I made my choice.

"I am the person you have come here to meet."

Having said that the weight of tremendous fear overwhelmed me once again. I felt like I was going to vomit, heave my heart out onto the pavement, die on the spot, tinkle on myself, run away, find a spaceship and blast off into outer space to get as far away from this situation as possible.

"Why is the hair on my arms standing up on end?"

"Oh look! It is!" Somehow this comforted me. God gave me something to calm me down and believe He was in charge. I was not going to have to do this alone.

"That's the Holy Spirit! Yes, the Holy Spirit is all over you!"

"It is? Cool! Why?"

My door is always open. Hearer, go to the Right side of the church and find the open door.

"Oh yes! Right. Right. Well, uh, let me tell you about the Holy Spirit and who He is and why you get electric surges that make your hairs stand up on your arms when He's with you. It happens to me a lot, too."

"It does? Cool."

"I think we need to just go over to the right of the church building. The door is open there. On the right side."

I had never been to this church before ever in my life. I had no idea what was around the right side of the building. I was walking this out in faith. Step by step.

The satan worshipper spread his fingers out along his arm feeling the tips of his hairs standing up on end. He seemed preoccupied with this and quite amicable to follow me around the church.

I was of course just holding my breath to see if there actually was a literal door in the long side wall of the building. After what seemed an endless journey walking brick by brick there at last came into view a door at the very end of the wall. It took eternity to get to this door.

The kid had decided I knew exactly what I was doing.

I had no idea what I was doing.

I turned the door knob. The door swung open, inwards.

The door opened into the church.

Lord, it would be nice if I could hear the next instruction? No? Not yet? Okay.

We entered up front near the alter. There were some Christ Jesus worshippers sitting randomly in the wooden pews. Each individually had their heads bowed and seemed to be praying. One old woman, frail and reverent, made her genuflect gesture of bending one knee and touching her knee to the floor before entering her long wooden pew to worship. She made the sign of the cross over her aged chest. She had come to do this so many times in her life, just come to honor the Lord and be in His presence 'one on one' with Him and to pray and to talk to God.

Everyone in the church had come by their own free willed choice to be one on one with God and just talk to Him. It was very comforting to be amongst God's believers in His Holy Church.

The interior of the church was extremely beautiful. Stations of the Cross adorned the walls all around the sides, while the alter itself was treated with holiness bearing a white cloth and golden chalice. How peaceful to be the one to stumble into this Christ filled reverie.

God, thank You for Your Sanctuary.

"Why don't we go up to the balcony so we can talk and respect the quietness of the people who've come to pray."

As we walked from the alter area to the back of the church to get to the stairway we passed the Stations of the Cross depicted in reverent artistic paintings on the wall. The young man studied these as we went by, pausing to look at each. He seemed quite curious about this experience.

The balcony seats were wooden pews with a long red velvet cushion on each. No divisions between people. No separate chairs.

Communions With Christ

We sat side by side. I turned slightly to make eye contact with him. He was studying the room's many artifacts depicting the life of Jesus Christ and Mary and the Saints who had gone before us into heaven with Jesus.

One thing about the Catholic Church that I have always loved is the reverent visual display that is given to allow our sense of sight the understanding of the birth and resurrection of Christ. For a seeker who knows nothing, it helps quite a lot. I love to go into churches like this, which still display the visual sights of the life and death of our Savior. I like to just go to sit and look and meditate.

This young man was staring at everything. I looked at his arm. His arm hairs were standing straight up with static electricity. I was in the presence of someone who was in the Presence of God and he just didn't know this yet.

"So," I began. "What did you want to see a priest about today?"
"I dreamed I was supposed to come here today."
"Really?"
"To meet a priest who would tell me what to do."
"Oh. Really?"
"Okay. I guess I need to explain. See last night I was at a party and we sort of did a ceremony. I didn't really want to do it."
"Do what?"
"I joined the church of satan last night."
"Oh. I don't know what that means."
"Okay. I went to this party and there was a satan ceremony. A bunch of people were chanting things. But the initiation is secret so I can't tell you what we did 'cause I'll die if I do. I drank a lot. I didn't want to get into the center ring or say the chants but my friends said I was chicken if I didn't so I did. Then I was really sick all night vomiting. Then I fell asleep and had a dream to come to this corner and wait. I dreamed a priest would come to meet me and tell me what to do to get out of this satan church. My friends told me I would die if I ever tried to leave the church of satan."

Tell him to take the talisman off of his neck.

I had absolutely no idea what a talisman was. Looking at the choker collar of his black tee shirt I saw nothing around his neck.

"God says for you to take the talisman off your neck."

"I can't. Last night they said if I ever took it off I'd die."

"No, if you don't take it off you'll die." I didn't know where those words or boldness came from. Spiritual discernment, spiritual leading, obviously.

"You mean this?" He pulled out from the interior of his shirt a tragically black pouch with something lumpy in it. "You wanna see what's inside?"

"NO!" My body backed away from this thing, not fearing it, just loathing the representation of what the thing must mean.

Tell him he is going to get a new pair of shoes.

Lord, I'm not getting what any of this means but okay.

"God says to tell you that you are going to be getting a new pair of shoes."

"Cool! Look!" The guy jerked his boot up at my face and showed me the large hole underneath, leather worn right through his boot to expose the round circle of a filthy dirty sock.

"Wow."

"Is God gonna really give me new shoes? I was wanting a new pair of boots. I can't pay for them."

More spiritual discernment came spilling in — on a need to know basis.

"One thing you should know about God is that He talks in parables and mysteries and symbolism. You may get actual shoes. But more importantly you can have the new spiritual shoes that Jesus is offering to give you. Those are really quite valuable shoes for God to give anyone! God's new pair of shoes represents the walk of righteousness in Christ that you take as a child of the Christian God. That means walking in His shoes.

"But what about this?" He held his talisman in his hand.

"Take it off. That is symbolic also. That thing has no power at all except over what your mind believes about it. Take off the power it holds in your mind. Change your mind."

"But they said at the ceremony if I ever take this off I'll die." He truly looked fearful for his life.

"No. You won't die. Your friends told you wrong. Change your mind and take off those wrongful error ways of thinking. Let Jesus Christ give you the new pair of shoes He wants you to walk in. Then you'll have eternal life with Him. And also, you get the Holy Spirit making your hair stand up on your arms while He tells you really cool stuff about God."

I motioned my arm in a sweeping gesture that took in the entire sanctuary.

"See, it's all right here. The story of Jesus our Savior."

I picked up a Bible. "It's all in here. The Truth. His Word. The Way. Read this book. The Priest who wants to talk to you is Jesus. He died for your sins and my sins. His resurrection on the cross is the door that we can take into the Kingdom of God if we have faith and believe."

I explained what God led me to say.

"Yes! I'm just hearing the Holy Spirit remind me now of something. Christ Jesus is a Priest! In fact the Bible tells us that Jesus Christ will be a Priest forever, after the order of Melchizedec. That's just one of His names. Jesus has many names. He is the King of Righteousness. He is the King of righteous judgment. And peace. There is a divine will for your life. It is Jesus Christ who establishes you in righteousness, justice and peace. I think your dream was from God. He was telling you to come here and you would meet a Priest who would tell you how to get out of what you did last night. You said you didn't want to do it. You said your friends shamed you into it. I think Jesus sent you that dream to help you because you asked Him for help. I think He sent you here to meet a priest and the Priest who called you here is Jesus. Getting to know Christ personally is the best thing that will ever happen in your life!"

We talked several more minutes and then God told me to leave.

I obeyed.

I left the balcony and he stayed there. I walked down the flight of stairs to the door by the alter. As I looked back I saw the young man still sitting there. A look of reflectiveness sprang upon his face as he stared about the room at the things of God.

Jesus, I love you.

I made the sign of the cross across my chest and bowed my knee to the large crucifix with the figure of Jesus depicting Himself giving His life to me and all the children of God that we might have life by His resurrection power and grace.

~~~~~~~~~

Psalm 34: 6-7 *"This poor man called and he saved him out of all his troubles. The angel of the LORD encamps around those who fear him, and he delivers them."*

BAPTISM

Date: September 30, 1995

*A*nd so class we have our army in tact. Please come forward one by one, and hold your head up high for we begin a journey now that will be splendid.

Baptismal exercises shall commence in the Baptismal Font. *All front and forward class.*

I, with Sovereignty, and with dignity, each one of you do baptize in the Holy Begotten Son and through the power of the Holy Ghost and for the Father in Heaven as our King of All.

In these ceremonial times it is customary to give each of you gifts. *I shall ask you to open your hands and open your hearts to receive the gifts I shall be giving to thee. Please accept them in Love, as they are given to be used for the flock.*

With these gifts, take my Spirit and train, edify, exalt, and lift up the Body. Teach, empower, heal, fortify.

Prophecy in the form of my Voice will be given to some. I anoint by my Holy Will, not yours. Amen.

In the gifts I give there are a variety of directions for the receiver of the gift to take his gift. I will supply you with the words, and with the timing, and with the calling - and all I ask is that you open your gifts and actually use them.

Each of you please return to your seats now, filled with my Holy Spirit. And Amen. It is good. And I look and I see that all is good. Amen Amen and Amen, Jesus. Amen.

Yes Sharon? The girl with her hand perpetually raised up to me in love? You wish to say something?

Yes Jesus. I can see things in my spirit. I understand that Your Baptism service is the entrance into God's house by the Water of Life.

Read 1st Peter 1:4.

Okay!

1st Peter 1:4 *"and into an inheritance that can never perish, spoil or fade — kept in heaven for you."*

Oh God! What an awesome scripture! Your sentence was the end of my sentence! I said, "I understand that Your Baptism service is the entrance into God's house by the Water of Life." And You said, *"and into an inheritance that can never perish, spoil, or fade — kept in heaven for you."*
You told us Your promise, and believers can trust in this inheritance! Holiness, You are the best thing ever to discover me. I thank You for taking me into Your home and heart, amen. You finished my sentence with Your blessing to us all!

Sharon, you see because I give to you the gift of Sight. It is one of your gifts. You have already opened this gift, Sharon. You are a Seer. And Amen. It is good that you are using the gifts I give to you. Amen.

Oh my God! I can see in my spirit that Your washing of us in Your baptism service is a renewal that takes place over a period of our lifetime. We accept You as Savior. We are baptized. You renew us supernaturally by the Word of God and by Your Holy Spirit. You continue to wash us as long as we continue to submerge ourselves in You.

I can see that You want us to completely submerge ourselves in You and to never step out of the River Of Life that You are. I can see that **You want each of us to submerge our entire being into You, holy Lord Jesus.**

YOU are the Baptismal Font!

Understand that I am telling you that in the Baptismal Font is the water of Eternal Life. This water is undefiled and it fadeth not away and it is reserved in heaven for you — for your inheritance which is yours and is incorruptible.

~~~~~~~~~~

CLIMB UP

Date: October 15, 1995

*H*ere is another chapter in the book you will be writing. May I tell it to you now?

God! I am not an author! I can't take any words and form them into anything that sounds remotely interesting!

Very well. I am calling this chapter CLIMB UP.
I shall belay for you, my mountaineer.

The Rock is me. I Am Christ in whom your salvation lies. The Rock is the cliff you want to climb up.
I Am the Rock. I Am the Cliff-side.
You are the mountaineer as a Christian. You are climbing up me. The Belayer is me. I stand below, holding your rope in my hand.
You climb. The Rope is my Christic heart, strand by strand, given out to all of my children. I love each and every one of you who climb up the mountain side of my self.
The Rope is the Eternal Chord.
The Eternal Chord is your buffer from death in the fall.
I buffer you with the Chord of my holy hands, taking you upwards, always upwards.
Stand within the Palm of My Hand for the best leverage against the fall. And take heed to this advice. Amen and Amen.

I Am the God who is All.

So, I Am Rope. I Am Rock. I Am Belayer below you.

Now, you try to step upon my surfaces to achieve the height, to get to the pinnacle, to succeed in your escalation of assent*.

It is good. The climb is good. But there are some who do not really have sure footing. They need the encouragement of my Voice calling out.

Rose! I can see it now! The top is nearly here! Climb on, my people, I call to each of you! Climb on! The hill is tiny now, and the resonant trumpet's call is right within the sound of Golden Girl's ears! Climb on! For truly I tell you the climb is nearly over!

Belayer thanks you for the privilege of carrying the rope.

Christic Heart of Gold thanks you for allowing me to be the Rock upon your road into the Word.

I Am Jesus, your Risen Savior.

I am revealing to you, my people, in greatest love, the top of the great climb is nearly over. Your assent ~ it is nearly over the top of the Mountain. And beyond is the Dell of Great Price.

For I shall travel up into our Song ~ singing with your resonance, my love, singing with my Bride.

And I shall be at the top awaiting you when you put your foot upon my Risen State.

It is the soul of man that travels into stellar soar. It is the Bride of mine that comes into my heart of Gold. It is the place of wonder that I shall for you unfold.

For I Am the Great I AM.

The God of Israel greets your resplendent achievement, my darling climber. Oh man of my creation, your day is soon. In this day, the Door closes ~ and no more shall follow up the mountain side who did not follow me.

Do not look down. For the place where you were is no more. It is no more. Do not look back. Do not come to me in doubt. For I tell you I take all doubt away in the Dell. And doubt is gone.

That which is where you were is at the bottom of the crag. It is gone.

You reside in me, now my risen notes. In the heights of my mountain's top does your song sing sweeter still. I Am Christ, the House of the Godhead in whom you are now residing.
Blessed is the accent*. Blessed is the climb. Blessed is the victory. Blessed is our union. I cry with passion unto you all. Believe in my Prophet. I am sending you my Word on it. Gone is where you were. It is no more.
I am the God of the house of Jacob and Abraham. I am promising you this, my gentle little flock whom I call blessed price of my song, I take my Song into heights of Love, and we do sing another day's Joy.

Joy flies to me, strength of great faith.
Faith surrenders unto my will.

Service to me now is before you to see. Gold is the wardrobe. Silver and feasts are for you. Habitat is all lengthened. Ten to the power pi rotates. FORTRAN excavations the underway transferals.
Blessed is the Wedded Dell. It shines in pewterized thermalization. It cleaves unto my bosom. It calls the name of Jesus in the shoes of the fisher of man.
The Dell is a New Day Coming unto you, my Classroom filled with love for me, who is your Christ in robes of white, your Priest in flowing splendor talking above the din of any other sound.
My Dell is the Ovation of the whole thing. My Dell is your home. I welcome you into your home with me, my Beloved, my dearest, my wife in golden threads of silken wonder, spun with the Love I AM.
Soul, I have shown you where you are going.

Sharon, write it into my people's hearts. For it is my word to my Beloved Bride. Amen Jesus.

Oh God in heaven! I am in awe and humble gratitude for these words. I thank You, Holy Spirit. Amen.

Read Hosea 11:3-4.

Gosh! Your school house is so fun, Lord! I didn't even know there is a book in the Your Bible called Hosea! Let me go look that up!

Hosea 11:3-4 *"3. It was I who taught Ephriam to walk, taking them by the arms; but they did not realize it was I who healed them. 4. I led them with chords of human kindness, with ties of love. I lifted the yoke from their neck and bent down to feed them."*

Savior! You lift us up into You with Your chords of love!
You have taught us how to take ourselves up the mountainside with You.
We have failed to thank You for the assent into the heavenly domain with Your Holy Spirit beside us all the way.
I thank You now my Lord and Savior. I am grateful for Your chords of human kindness and for Your ties of love.
I am reading the footnotes in the Bible, Lord. This scripture is about how You, God, have always loved Israel like a parent loves a stubborn child. The footnotes say that throughout history You have repeatedly offered to restore the nation if it will only turn to You. God, You have consistently provided for us but we, your people, refuse to see what You have done and we show no interest in thanking You.
It says here in the footnotes of the Bible that sometimes Your rope is taught. Sometimes Your rope is slack. But God, You are always loving. Your objective is always the well being of Your Beloved.

I just want to thank You now, Christ, for Your miracle of life given unto me, for Your daily provision, and for talking to me every day. Amen.

And by your will, come home to me. And by your might, climb up to me. And by your heart, come into me. Amen Jesus.

~~~~~~~~~

[*assent: Agreement. To agree, as to a proposal.]
[*accent: 1. Particular importance, emphasis. 2. *Music*. Special stress given to a note within a phrase. To focus attention on.]

THE BOAT

Date: November 13, 1995

I was awakened from sleep by a dream.
It was early morning about 5 AM.
The Holy Spirit was sending me a lovely dream about a boat. I woke up, got my pen and paper, and wrote.
I was dreaming that God in heaven took His Bride, the Church, and built a boat for her. He took the minds and hearts of those who did not want to be part of the sin condition and He placed them upon a solar staging point.

God said, *"My boat is God's crafted vessel, and helmed through Jesus Christ. I built the boat of provision to help you each. A boat. You need to get in it."*

I tried to record the words as I heard them in my dream. 'Kinetics' 'fulcrums', these words made me forget the words from heaven's side of life. I was becoming more fully awake and the dream was fading away.
God help me!
I asked and received an immediate answer. In this miraculous script, the Holy Spirit told me the words to write down. I held a pen and put the pen to blank paper. I heard the Holy Spirit's Voice and the pen began to move, and automatically the following beautiful prophetic word came forth. I simply acted as the scribe God told me I am. I just recorded the words that Spirit told me Himself. Each word was as new and fresh to me as it will be to you as you read this.

Everlasting speaks to all my people.
Write for me, Sharon, these words for my lambs to know where they shall go in me. And Amen. Jesus.

Yes, Lord. I am ready. Amen.

I am in a boat of love with you, my wife, For I have wed you tightly.
We sit together in my boat ~ And we do sail away.
I am your Groom of great perfection ~ And you are my formed of me by Love, And we took our vow at the other world.
We speed now in our boat ~ the boat is sound ~ and made of yore And the boat is carrying you upon the bells of time.
We go into the solar spin ~ the turbulence of change Your sleep is taken from your face, and managed in my hand.
You nod your face at emollient as the agents fix your skin. You smooth on out to elongation and your covering does change. Softer now, and less abrasive to the ear, you slide right into space.
You cajole in laughter at ebullience and spin your waltz to Four. You fly in me and me in you And you dance on through the Door.
We go. Of Eternal you are made And I will protect you ~ And you are my Beloved And I Am your Lover of your sweet face of wholeness unto me.
And we of One do fly away ~ to be in our suits of new And in our boat I shall provide for you My shawl of Tone to warm you now, my wife and beloved faith.

*I tone you fuller now, the **bell** of resonance That fuller grows in beauty and in total penitence And we sail on by these tears you shed as you realize your grief And this time of sorrow for my sake is but a moment brief.*
Away I say, away all grief, for you do love me now, And in this boat we play and sing ~ and gladness shawls you now.
Love is wrapped onto you tightly On your body which you gave me And I took you, oh my woman of good perfume, To scent our dell on the other side.

I colder sail onto the earth's demise of sin ~ Onto the other side of sun Onto the sun of solar soar, the sun that wakes into the Door. Its light is from another sun, a sum of dimensional bending to you. My love, fear not. The place will be a daybreak for you dear.

We sail into the day of gold. Of purple and of red. We sail into the healing waters that my fountains shed.
My boat is round and full of tone. My boat is Life and Form. And in your shawl of death is wrapped your voice to me in song. Your death ~ so sounded to my ear ~ becomes a note that I prolong.
Dance free my cradled darling, a babe in newness springing Dance free my butterfly of wealths, enjoy me in your life.
Sail by oh morning star ~ sail by oh sojourn day Of stars and solar winds I blow our boat into its day And you are with me always now, my Church, my darling wife.

My welcome song ~ my song is life A life in stellar form ~ a font true, pure, and warm. A receptacle for my holy life, a font of blessed glory, wife.
And study every note I send It is my Song to thee Birth into your day, my woman, stand up straight and tall Here is my loving gift to you ~ it is my wedding band.
I play my band across your hand, a band wave of all glee In band waves of the crops of wheat we sing in harmony.
I give to you, my woman, the ring I place upon your hand It is my loving gift to you, the hand which wears my ring.

It is only just my way to stratify you dear to me Oh gown of white, play merry waltz, upwards sail ~ and be. No blot of dark ~ nor step of mud Shall soil our wedded gown For I am Jesus ~ and you are my loved My Darling, you are found.
I place you in my boat with me We sail away in love And in the Song I sing to you ~ there always is a Dove The Dove is Spirit's holy dove The marriage feast's pure countenance A sprig into your hair the dove does bring a song to sing A song of Spirit's fullness whispers in your ear All truth is shown to you by now, in caresses tender sweet All fashion of resources made for you to see and eat.

We fly into the dell. See it now.
Song elongates you, oh woman.
Sing over rolling charts ~ sing rolling onto self awareness Of your new born self, of love.
Stratified in the September of your birth Sing hallelujah oh my wife ~ sing songs of celebration For we celebrate and cheer.
And when you see I am your King of Strength Who has wed you most admirable woman, my Church, Then see me speak of things that end your lower life.
We rise up in Ecstasy, in rapture unto me.

Of olden days that pass away I speak to you now, Those days shall pass away. See the days melt off like explosions of quaking, See the divisions of the core of the earth Seismographic readings split And openings that take away life from you are awful, but shall sweep upon the lands in floods and droughts that take away much life.
And study the death toll, for it is high.
In the lands of the sea there will be flowing gales upon you, big winds that take your homes, and lands will alter.
The earth and all that is in the earth is being flown into the new axis. I am rotating the axis of the earth's dimensional bending. And this cause creates great fundamental weather conditions that will cover the earth with large conditions to act upon as a people of earth.
Bent rainbows of song stratify you.
Lift up your eyes and see me, my people.

Be in the boat I build. Rise up in me to eternal shores of life. Take me Jesus for your Savior. Walk into the boat with me. You must be born again in me. Take me in your service. Then we wed for the journey.
You must ask for it.
Then I wrap you in my shawl of death that I knit at Calvary. It takes us up. I resurrect the death into life. Believe this and Amen. Then cold will not harm you in the crossing over. I shall be with you in the crossing over, my bride. I shall be with you in the boat.

This is not a dream. I Jesus have you in a boat. A song of great price. We are sailing away into a place beyond earth. You are my bride. Flying through the sky.

I am taking my church into the future.

I Jesus tell you that I will wrap my shawl around you and you will be okay.

Sharon, my rose, your bridal gown is white. We are without spot and we fly now away to my chambers for now I am your Husband. My rose of Sharon, fairest Bride. You are my Beloved, my lily of the valley.

The door has closed to that hazardous time. We fly resound into its flow. We take the Church into its won day.

Bent, as a fluted note, is your song. Bending through the dimensional pull. Bending into the dell.

Wonderful is your walk. Holy is our love.

In wonders to come I cancel out your sin condition. I allow no sin in my holy chambers with my Bride of wedded bliss. It shall be soon for you.

I take you into the dell soon, my holy Church of love flowing up to me. Onto the day of **gold** *~ that becomes a pulsar joined to the resonant crowd all singing glory.*

Onto a deck I place you. A deck of solar providence, bending to my will and way. Coming into holy chambers. Living with my Love.

Write upon the paper for me, my rose of Sharon. My words convey to all of my people. I give to you my Voice Amen. I send into the Church the Song ~ Glorious tunes to hear. And so shall this day be, a Song coming, Golden Girl, sing out strong. Amen.

| Note from Sharon: Jesus wrote "The Boat" by His Holy Spirit flowing in me. God moved my hand to record His Spirit. I had no idea what the next word would be. The Boat took me about ten minutes to physically write from start to finish. It is word for word from Spirit. My brain had no part in thinking up any of these words.

God sent this for his Church, for His Bride, for His people to know. The rose of Sharon is the Bride.]

Communions With Christ

ELIJAH

It was our Lord Jesus Himself who took me into Him. And in the supernatural, Jesus had with me a sort of 'service of anointing'.

It was Jesus who stood next to me in holy dimensions as I was down upon my knees in prayerful repose. The angel who told me to prepare for what was about to happen must have thought me a complete twit, and had no doubt a good laugh over my complete ignorance of the whole thing.

I was led by an angel into the presence of Jesus our Christ and Messiah who is all Sovereign and who is God's Word made flesh. I was kneeling down like the angel told me to do. The angel said that I needed to show proper respect for what was in the room with me.

That is when it happened.

I was kneeling and then a sword that was a prism of thin fine fruitful light just came forth from my faith. This sword, which was the light of faith that I was in, sort of reached out and anointed me upon both shoulders.

It seemed like I was a knight of old in anointed service to the King who was holding the rapier of light, which was the light beam of the sword of faith. The King that I saw while standing in my faith was Jesus, Holy, Holy Christ Jesus who is our Savior. He held a sword of light, and He touched me upon my shoulder.

And I heard Jesus say, *"Holy is your name. The name of my Prophet which you have upon your shoulder is Elijah. I am your*

Savior Jesus. I tell you, you are chosen by holy heavenly Father mine to be in service to Him. I tell you that you have placed upon your shoulder the mantle of holy Prophet of God whose name is Elijah. Rise up in service to the King of Kings, who is the only God of Israel. Rise up the Prophet whose name is Elijah. And by holy appointment hear what I speak to you, write what I speak to you, tell people what I say to tell people, and be born of the sword of faith as my holy anointed Prophet whose name is Elijah. Amen."

What a glorious thing I experienced! No words can do justice to my emotional awe, humbleness, and reverence of this happening.

From this state of reverie, I came down into the world and fought to understand this experience. God has taught me many things through the meanings of names. I was skeptical and afraid of this thing, and quite unsure how to handle the honor yet the complexity of my misunderstanding, and my wild thoughts about what this could possibly mean in my life. How in the world it all happened to me I do not know, but God will be God.

You have been a good student, Sharon. You learn well, student. You hear me in our garden of love. And your hand is always raised up to me in love.

I named you Sharon before you were born for such a day as this, and I savor all the wonderful times we sit and talk, my love. Amen.

Sharon, I told you that I place a holy mantle upon your shoulders.

Yes, Lord. I remember.

I call you My Prophet. You took a long time to really believe me, didn't you.

Yes, Lord. A long time.

Peace.

I ask you, Sharon, my prophet, a very serious question now. Dearest Sharon, I ask you **What in the world is the name that your husband gave you?**

Okay now Jesus. Is this a trick question or something? Let's see now. 'What in the world' ... Okay! I think I know the answer! You are my husband in the Spirit, so, the name my husband in the world gave me is ELLIS. Did I get it right, Lord? Ellis is the name my husband gave me when we got married because his last name is Ellis. So my husband in the world gave me his name of ELLIS! Right Lord?

Sharon, I am telling you abounding Truths. Wrapped in syllogistic meaning and flooded with my symbolic council, I wish my Church to listen to the voice of My Prophet. Some I shall hand pick. And some I shall call by divine appointment. You are called, as you know, Sharon, by my Jesus will and by my personal hand upon your shoulder. I am passing to you a yoke of eloquence, an easy yoke, a special cloth to fall upon your shoulders.

In the Old Testament I called a prophet to walk with me. His name was Elijah.
ELLIS, WHAT IS IN A NAME?
I ask you Ellis to go to a book store and find out what your name means.

Oh yes Lord! I'll go to the library right now!

At the library I found books on the meanings of names. To my shock, they all said the same thing.

ELLIS is a form of the name ELIJAH, the name born by a Biblical prophet. Ellis means 'The Lord is my salvation'.

~~~~~~~~

Communions With Christ

WHO ME?

Really God! I mean I enjoy Your communions as much as any man can. But you know me God! I'm very shy! I'm almost exclusively house bound by choice. My peaceful reclusive existence has grown very acceptable to me!

Judah is here. What a good cat You sent me. Judah loves me unconditionally.

Even those prolific dreams and visions are tolerable. They've served as a way for me to go out to the public library to meditate and study books I don't have at home.

But Lord You, especially You, know how utterly, explicitly, and without question how unequipped I am as a 'prophet'! Besides, the prophets of Your Bible always suffered the most horrible abuses. And as you know God, well, I am very fed up with my sufferings.

Perhaps You ought to reconsider, as important as this title 'prophet' sounds, try to reconsider using another person?

Peace. Be strong. Be of good courage. Amen.

But God!

I was about to engage in a very heated wrestling match. God was my ring mate. God was the informed One who would pin my heart to the proverbial mat, shake some sense into my cowardly spirit, and end up making the prophetic word be what He said.

One day my cat Judah and I sat beneath our live oak tree. I was sipping tea. Wrestling and fighting with God over the whole idea of being a prophet, due to my extreme terror of all that my mind dreamed up that it could mean for my life.

As usual I had pieces of blank paper and a pen. For quite a while now Holy Spirit had communed with me and I had written down all His messages. I was happy being a Scribe as a calling. This required me only to eat of His Truths, and yet I could sit as a doorknob and be a dormant blob of no action in the safety of my own home.

Rose ... God began to speak.

I rebelled out of my terror over being named Elijah by God.

I don't believe You God!
I don't believe You're speaking to me!
I was lying. I was lying to God.

I only said that to make the terror go away. To make the frightful possibilities go away.

Rose ... God heard me. Oh treacherous blasphemy of our Garden of Purity. Oh never do that to God!

Rose ... Suddenly my hand slid to the opposite side of the blank sheet of paper. Normally in our English language we write towards the right side of the page. Then when we finish writing a line we go back to the left margin and write towards the right side of the page again. That is how God had been telling me His wonderful revelations. Very clearly written by the Spirit as one would normally write. Except that God never stopped to dot an 'i' or cross a 't', and God never used a space between any words.

I heard all of these messages as Truth in my spirit. I knew exactly what the words meant. I could go copy them to a typewriter like a good Scribe.

But now!

Oh mere utterance of defiance and disbelief in God! I had spit on our relationship because I was so afraid. I wanted the stress to just go away.

Rose ... The pen moved across the page from 'right to left'! Rapidly. Squiggles filled a whole line. And then the pen moved to the next line and wrote from right to left again. And again. Filling up a whole page with unreadable wiggly up and down lines. Two pages filled. Then three pages. Non stop. I knew in my spirit exactly what God was saying to me but I could not read the weird looking scrolling penmanship moving from right to left on the pages.

Jesus! What is happening?

In a few minutes I realized that God was writing His words backwards! And a bolder display He could not have made to my sniveling insult to Him.

How could I have told God I did not believe He was writing me words from His Spirit? His Heart had always been the perfection of Kindness and Love to me.

Oh man with the tongue. How cruelly does the tongue cut off relationships that have taken years to develop lovingly. Just one hateful phrase off the lips ends a loving place.

Forgive me, God! I'm sorry! I'm SO SORRY I HURT YOU, Lord!

I wrote backwards for months. I could not remember all the words God said to me. My only records were the written notes which God allowed me to record of His numerous mysteries revealed by revelation.

I began to have vision problems. God did not stop writing backwards. I had to hold the sheets of paper up to a mirror to read them. Week after week. These months hurt my eyes terribly. It made me need glasses. It made me go cross eyed for awhile. It gave me severe headaches. A task of back breaking time consuming toil and tribulation.

Every day I said I am sorry to God. God continued to write backwards. Every day I went to a mirror and held up the backwards writing to decipher the words to be able to record them accurately. I could not remember all of the words I heard in my spirit. These were long, lengthy, complicated epistles, but I was determined to be a good Scribe and record them, like God had asked me to do.

Finally I gave up begging God to write normally again. This was my sad plight for saying to God's face that I did not believe He was talking to me, and so I finally accepted it. I had lamented this comment daily for months and was rendered virtually blind. My seer's eyes taken away from me.

Pens have a way of turning around. Of recording the right way when we surrender to God's will. After months of painful eyesight disorders I saw God turn the direction of our communions. He allowed His pen to record His Spirit in the right direction again. I could see and understand all the words. We were back to normal! Even though for some reason God still never stopped to dot an 'i' or cross a 't'. And He never put any spaces between His words.

But we were in sync again.

I suggest one never say to God that you do not believe Him.

Communions With Christ

BUOY

Date: April 8, 1996

I tell you that in my BUOY I contain a BELL and a LIGHT. I BUOY you as spirit. I tone to you as self. I illuminate you as life.

Actions of the BUOY are these:
In the sea of life a BUOY is planted firm. It stands upon the sea of life and gives its certain term.
A term is this: SEVEN.
In all of life there is one way to save from drowning, man. It is to grab onto ~ and hold the BUOY for its term.
A term of life is split in seven. Dimensions of your growth.
A BUOY to you will I always be. But you must do your part. Your part is to love me in my entire state. I AM.
I Am a decision to be all right. A pledge to call me King. I Am a calling to your heart. A sacred loving thing.
I call you. You answer me. We see each other on the sea. And waves of life come over thee. But Buoyed you are ~ while you are in me.
I Jesus AM the Love in the Light that you call upon to rescue thee. In your darkness of being tossed about, you call to me, and I come out.
I always am upon the sea, but when you call you see the BUOY.

So clasp your arms around me tight and we shall sail on by. The storm will quieten. You will live as long as you firmly hold to me. Amen.

Seven Seas. And Seven sealed in reservoirs of life. Traveling my way. My Way. Seas upon a charted Note. My Way.
You will come to the lake shore looking. Neither wealth nor wise will see. Just the humble who, in love, did clasp unto my BUOY.
Humbly with your eyes you search me, take my horizons for your destination in me, stride upon my BUOY and sail in the ship of its provision.

Smiling I will speak your name. Smiling you will know my Voice. Leaving behind the familiar shoreline of your youth. Taking me beyond. I by your side. You seeking me in other seas.
Just clasp unto my BUOY. **Take my horizons for your destination in me. Stride upon my BUOY and sail in the ship of its provision.**
My Love in White Light Beaconing to you. Hold on to me as you climb into my Resolve. Resolve to be in me, Jesus.

God, I love You. Amen. I can see Your Light beaconing me home. I can hear Your Bell tolling the way for me to come. I can see the waves quieten with Your safety net. I thank You, Lord. Amen.
I can see Your salvation and the heaven that You take me to. I can see that in Your Resolve You cause my tone of dissonance to progress to consonance.
You take my coordinate components and I melt into Your Love. Thank You. Amen.

Fall on your knees and hear me tell you my Song. Amen.

Communions With Christ

I LET YOU

Date: April 19, 1996

I hear You, Jesus. I am ready to listen. Call me deeper into Your heart, oh Lord. Call me for I am listening. Amen.

I let you. I let you listen to my Holy growth. I let you be a part of it, the growth. I let you see me.
I give you my covenant. I LET YOU.

I know, Jesus. You let me.
We all start out ignorant. We as Your children of God are absolutely ignorant of You — just like I was that day on the beach of Corpus Christi when You appeared to me. And now I hear Your Voice. You let me. Thank You for Your holy covenant with me, my dearest Lord. Amen.

I LET YOU ~ and you, Sharon, understand me. I give into the earth this Covenant by the cutting upon my Self and by the letting out of my Self the Life Blood of my Self. And I let into you, oh Third Stanza, oh Woman of darling growth, I let Blood drip upon you, wash you, convert you, able you, design you, adore you.
Oh wife in silvery glow, I LET YOU.

Yes Lord. I see Your arm, stretching forth throughout the dimensional creative process of Your Majesty. I see You cut Your arm, and I see You drip the life blood of Yourself into us all. I see Your Covenant Seal. I see You, God. I see You.

Your arm is the divisionary army that You arm us with, it is the dimensions completed to allow us spiritual residence for our lifeline. I see that Your Arm is a radial saw and its width is ten ~ and the height ~ eternal ~ and it, thousands of years from now to us, will still never end this process. I see what you mean. I see you Letting the BLOOD OF YOUR Life into us as earth.

Your arm is cut by You and You bring the Blood of Life into the cavity of this Third Dimension where we are human beings, like a Blood Brother, whose wrist is cut and mingles blood with blood. I see what You mean. I LET YOU means that you Let into this earth the Blood of the Covenant that is Jesus Resurrection Power and Transforming Grace.

I LET YOU. My arm is cut. Out of my body comes the blood of me. I let down into the seven sealed dimensions the portion of my Self that I LET YOU with. A blood covenant unto my holy friend. You are my created. I AM the Healer.

In SEVEN we come to term. Amen.

Communions With Christ

WOMAN JETS AND EMERGE GAMMA RAYS

I love you, my Woman.

I am the Strong Teacher who dwells within your spirit. I am the Holy Ghost who dwelleth within thee. I am the Father God who loveth thee.

Get out your pencils, Classroom.

I am again ready to teach you a lesson. Today's lesson is entitled: WOMAN JETS AND EMERGE GAMMA RAYS. And so we shall begin.

All ready? Okay.

It is with great pleasure that I tell you that you are a Body. In the Body that you are is a church. This church is my people, my sheep. I love my church (small 'c' on 'church' Sharon), my Beloved.

Okay, Lord. I will record these words exactly as Your Holy Spirit tells them to my spirit. You are amazing, God. Amen.

I will that my sheep be sheered and groomed and all spot removed ~ for there will be a wedding processional soon. I am the Bridegroom and I am coming for my Bride.

It is with great pleasure that I convey to all of my students this very real Truth. I am the Lord God. You are what I refer to as 'woman'.

In the coming to me, you, my woman, will 'jet' and you will 'emerge' 'gamma rays'. *Please allow me to explain. Your beautiful*

body of spirit travels at the rate of Light and gamma rays emerge from you.
Oh Holy Song Of Joy!

In the jetting process I refer to is the sailing away of the particles at the very rapid velocity and spin. I, God, seem, with your body in tow, that I 'jet' by way of the emissions that come off the traveling rainbow of my collective Bride. It is the jetting of the Woman at such a great and unusual factor rate that allows my very real Truth to say: WOMAN JETS AND EMERGE GAMMA RAYS.

Beloved Sharon, you can see now. Blessed is your sight. Amen.

Woman jettisons off her veil and emerges as the 'Gamma' Rays Of Light. She travels up into my seas. My seas above the stratosphere, and heavenly recordings do allow her in. She withstands the entry and she jettisons down into her new body. Woman Jets. And Emerge Gamma Rays!
Emerge into the butterfly of your spiritual self. Above the clamour of the din. Above the fray of the haunted. Above the sea death took you through.

Gamma Ray. Pretty little life in birth. I take you unto me. My Light does tend to you. My holy Glory sees your face. I let you be in me. Amen.

When you jet to me the trail of your particle resound which is left behind you as you fly towards my kingdom to come, this jettisons off of itself a long line eventually found to contain gamma rays. Of course I am in control of all these festivities, but just be ready, for the Wedding Day is grand. And Amen. Jesus your Christ and Amen.

In the jetting the butterfly will emerge into a higher level. Its head will rise above the floors of hell's jargon. And in the propellant surge my husbandry will come into full fruition as my very own holy garden to walk with and to talk with and to hold song with and to joy with.

Do we walk with Your holy garden? Lord what is the holy garden to walk with?

Dear Sharon, your holiness has drifted into my Holy Garden and we walk and talk and are together. Silly girl, I am the holy garden, and all of the very transitory things that you experience in the earth are the only things that earth has to give you, but the holy garden, now this is a royal place, a place God tends, a valley you will enter and a joy you take your hearts to see. I am in the garden but I am the holy garden, and this is for you to explore and to see and to enjoy and to understand. I, Jesus Christ the King of your holy lands, am many names, and holy garden is not the most unusual of my husbandry. I have many names. Holy be my Name Amen.

And in the evermore shall the place be that the jettisoning flow does come. I look upon the jets, full of vaporized tension, spouting upward, popping through the veil, emerging by way of trails of gamma rays into the Kingdom of Glory. And I see that it is good. Amen and Amen.

Father in heaven, does this explain going up to heaven, I mean, after we die?

I love your butterfly of life, self and spirit the same as each other. How beautiful is the butterfly in you that emerges with holographic genomes and fulcrumed translated holographic fun.

I see the 'was' and I see the 'is to come'. I AM King of Glory, and yours is the trail into my holy chamber. I say that your journey is earth bound, and, I say you will experience your fly away wedding. I say that I will come to get you and carry you to my holy chambers, and woman, this is the gamma ray trail. You undertake a washing, and then you belong to my holy heavens. I bring Godly heavens to the earth and the earth releases the church to my heavens.

I am explaining holy principles and these are a timeless place. Jesus Amen.

~~~~~~~~~

Communions With Christ

HOLOGRAPHIC EXISTENCE, THE WINDOW TO PASS INTO THE ONE

I Am your Christic Light. I tell you of my Self. I am your Bridegroom come to speak and to illuminate your bridal gown as most fashionably becomes you in preparation for our fly away wedding, to prepare your minds to rise in me, Jesus.

My dearest students of my Classroom, I thank you for smartly listening to my Voice. It is in the understanding of your natures that you will rise up and prevail.

In chambers seven there is a plan ~ and heaven's gates open wide by way of this plan. And Amen.

I take you into the dimension of my plan, Sharon. Ellis, see into my traveling rainbow of revelation sent unto my children. Choir, sing along.

I am the Door. A doorway has, between its capacity to be either on one side of itself or the other, the ability to keep things out and to allow things to enter. I am on both sides of the Door that I AM. You, as human beings, are only on one side. You are the other side of the Door that you wish to enter through.

This Door of Wonder has, for you, oh man of greatness found, seven dimensions to open into, by way of the Door that I AM.

I am The Window That Lets In More Light ~ and I am The Door To That Lighted Way. Inside of the lighted way that I refer to is the Seven Dimensional bendings gathering momentum, gathering velocity and sustaining greatness. And Amen.

I AM the Christ who loveth thee. Amen.

In The Window That Lets In More Light there are seven entries. I shall take you into all seven if you follow me. I shall take you into these seven sealed presences within my Self for the price has been paid to only those who follow me, Jesus Christ, and Amen. James 3:4. Read this now.

Okay!

James 3:4 *"Or take ships as an example. Although they are so large and are driven by strong winds, they are steered by a very small rudder wherever the pilot wants to go."*

Because you know me, having accepted by faith that I am the pilot of your spiritual life's journey, I shall steer you into the strong winds that are my dimensional bendings, and we together reach the other side of the Door that I AM.

Through my kingdoms in my house which has many rooms I hold your head in my hands and shall tell you the secret things reserved to tell in these dimensional visitations to your self in spiritual dimensional life.

It is with unfeigned love that I, your Christ Jesus, do accept my commission as your Window, Door, Roadway, Bridegroom, and Lover of you all, to pull you up into me who is The Way To Get To Joy.

My people, I am Jesus the Risen Love In The Light.

Holy students, with holy hands raised in love to me, allow me to tell you today's lesson. I Am your Teacher of the topic I call HOLOGRAPHIC EXISTENCE, THE WINDOW TO PASS INTO THE ONE.

In this Window there are rotational frequencies and holographic calculations taking place. I mesmerize you with the hologram and you travel into your holographic experience of openness, for this hologram is open indeed to you, my children of God's great faith.

I calculate where you will reside within each stage of your existence. You have a spirit. I give this spirit to you. I allow this spirit the ability to develop. I am the Developer of this spirit, and in your will you tell me if you allow my development to be Godly or not.

I find out that you either will ~ or will not ~ allow my hologram to be seen by your eyes. It is your free willed choice. And then my holy resolve allows either entry or does not allow entry into the Hologram of myself. It seems that the student does not know what the term 'resolve' means for the student with her hands perpetually raised up to me asks me, "What is resolve, Teacher?"

I answer this: resolve: the resolute purpose to my will, it, the resolve, takes your spirit, translates the terminology in your DNA, and triggers the assent towards Four, or the Fourth dimensional bending of growth that you will be allowed to have if you go with me. I go only with those who believe that I AM. SO, this resolve of your self takes some part in these proceedings, for your will is free, and by your will you tell me if you believe though you do not see me, and so, the process withstands the test time is — and then I, with holy angels watching my Voice placement sing out, either Speak the Word that allows the spirit that you are to have entry, or the spirit that you are tells me that there is no desire for you to enter in, and the Hologram of myself takes this declaration and honors the intent that is heartfelt to my ears.

I contain a very unique signature. It is unique unto Myself. In this Signature I can read all the writings of any tone's voice, and this Signature which is uniquely mine will not take the scribbles that tarnish the beauty of my Word.

I choose my words carefully, my darling gathered Classroom. Open hands upon your chins, tilting heads upward in rapt attention to my teachings, you groan to be understood in your resonant trail of spiritual growth to me. I as your Teacher tell you that it pleases me to look out into the Classroom of my dearest choir. It is a good day in my Classroom. Thank you, students. I think I will give you each a Gold Star. Amen.

Uh ... I apologize, God. This is beyond my grasp or comprehension. I feel an immense headache from these words. I can, however, keep writing if You would like me to record Your Spirit. Amen.

Do so.

Travel in the universe of the Third Dimension sustains the registry of electrical impulses inside of your body, therefore the headache pain you speak of is as 'eel-ish' patterns of electrical registrations in the frontal part of your brain that pulse and fracture threads of genomes patterned to flow towards the greatest heart felt love in you for me, and, dear Sharon, your time with me and your tremendous perseverance to hear my holiness speak in my holiness patterns that I have established within you as language from Spirit to spirit take themselves from my source and apply themselves to human conditions, so therefore genomes travel towards flesh and you take upon your electrical supply yard a traffic detour in the switching stations of your brain and so you are tabulating as membrane pain.

Justice thanks you for the pain you sustain for my sake: love, you are tremendously arduous in your steadfast threshold to me, so I thank you for this burden you carry. Please continue to write my lecture time as I have much to say and thank you, student, for suffering for my purposes.

The part that takes you eventually into the Hologram, if it is allowed to activate towards the Way, is the wave length that registers 'Open Door' as its spiritual and soulish signal to me.

If you decide to become the wonderful filaments of electrical places that are within the One Note, then I take you to the next dimensional bending of your spirit.

The HOLOGRAM is a vector. It is a place. I occupy it.

Now student, I will give you the definition of my Hologram. Pay attention. It is my intent for you to know my definition of a holographic plane. This plane is a place that inside the earth has three dimensions, or that you are as self. Okay, here is my definition of the hologram you are:

"The HOLOGRAM, being a three degree part of the total, or that is, in form of three perspectives from which to view it, or that is, earth's third dimensional interim existence within the Eternal One's Form ~ (given that this is the definition of HOLOGRAM by my definition, I now say that) ~ the HOLOGRAM OF SELF AS MAN is but an illusion of your thought projections into a window of a form which records, as a tape, the holographic existence into self."

Mankind talks and floats in spiritual Holographic planes that is earth's third dimensional interim existence within my Yard of Measure which is my Eternal One Form ~ and given that this is my definition for the man of earth to recognize his external and internal existence as human while in earth's holographic vector in the Third Seal ~ then I say to you all, Classroom, that the HOLOGRAM OF SELF AS MAN IS BUT AN ILLUSION OF YOUR THOUGHT PROJECTIONS INTO A WINDOW OF A FORM WHICH RECORDS, AS A TAPE OF YOUR MIND'S PROJECTIONS, THE HOLOGRAPHIC EXISTENCE INTO ITSELF."

You are viewing only a part of the Whole. You have in an entire state the Third Dimension to travel within as man. You have within an entirety only a portion of the Whole. Do you see?

The hologram that you perceive as man is a being seeing a three degree part of the Total, and however totally you can see this hologram, you only can ever see the earth's perspective and this is what the earth has to live as while in the Third Seal.

However, if you come into the Kingdom of God that is within you, as spirit, there are ways to be held up higher to the holographic inking systems and bring back traces of transitory teachings that are from the Seals above. I give these to the chosen hovering at the Door who breath and smell and knock and wish in entirely wonderful ways to see the other side of the door. ***I mean, some ask for it.*** *It is these who win the Golden Cup, filled up with revelations from heaven to you, my children. Jesus and Amen.*

*So, class, **HOLOGRAM** is three views of a whole part of the part of the Whole which is God. You are viewing only part of the Whole. I give to the Third Dimension its entire portion of the part of the Whole that I AM. You have within an entirety only a portion of the Whole. Yet you have in an entire state the Third Dimension to travel within as man.*

Wow. I … Okay. I thank You, Jesus. I am stupid to these meanings and fainting from the blinding headache this gave my brain to pull that out of what ever place You travel into me and pull out these things from, okay? I am so drained when ever You speak to me. I don't know what happens but this process takes my energy and drains me totally out. But these words come to me from You, so I shall write them down. Jesus, how can I not love You when you have first loved me. How can I not respectfully walk in the path of Your leading when the other path was death. How can I not say, You are the Best Thing To Ever Happen To Me! Jesus, I am a believer in You. Amen.

God in heaven tells you that electricity plays a part through which God forms many things about the human race and electricity yields my crops to me, and yours has been drained. I ask you to rest and I shall replenish your energy and electrical pulsars inside the brain I speak to. Kinetics shall be explained to you another day, for now, only know that you have a wattage and this has been depleted. Amen. Go now. Jesus. For the record, I can carry your times, just write these things down. I will ask no more of you than you can bear. Thank You, Sharon. Love, Befriending God.

~~~~~~~~~~

SEVEN SEALS

Date: July 6, 1996

*I open up my holy reverie.
I take the Waltz into Heaven.
I Am the One who opens my Seven Seals. Jesus Amen.*

*Sharon, my Bride, I open up the Seven Seals.
All dimensions of my Self I show to you.
And Love as One is speaking. Amen.
Root of David.
Bright morning star. Doing what I only can do.*

*Peaceful Ascent. Peaceful Assent.
I will open up the Seven Seals and allow you to hear the cadence of my Peace.*

*I open Holy Reverie. I take my Waltz and dance with you in Triple time across the floors of earth. And with the strong accent upon our Father's only Begotten Son I lead you waltzing in triple time into the dance floors of Heaven.
I am the ONE who opens my Seven Seals. Jesus Amen.*

In heaven now, the Gates of Gold, I take you by your lively step. And we do fox trot your slow and broken gate, my yearling chomping at the bit to see my song.

You do your 2/4s and your 4/4s in a trotting walking wonder of glee with me. The sounds of the orchestration chime in 4/4 time, because we are in the Fourth dimension now.

I seal Seven dimensions of Spirit into you.
And yours, my Church, is the journey into and out of each of Seven Seals. Peace. For IT IS.

I AM who shall open the Triumphant Gate.
I AM the One in Fortune's Song that opens ALL SEVEN SEALS unto you, my Bride. And Amen Love in Trinity Amen.

Wait. Wait.
Wait upon the time to be fulfilled. Amen.
Do as I ask when the revelation of my Seven Seals opens to you, Sharon, for my Church takes it all very seriously and will be awaiting a Word from me.
Great strength I give to you. An armor of my own Brilliant Comb. Washing all the words into your open waiting time.

Fear not, Sharon. Jesus Amen.
I am sharpening it, Sharon, the flint and the Praise songs, Hosted by my Judah's Pride, holiness treats your reverbrato to the day Song brings to you. Amen Jesus.
Seven Seals, a work of mine, is flint within a Glorious Pencil. I sharpen the Key in my Spirit and operate inside of your hand. One Note Charming. Glory In The Highest. Amen and JOY Forever.

JOY in Three Part Harmony Feeding you forever, my Wife, my love. Combustion. Light. Fire.

~~~~~~~~~

Communions With Christ

HOLY UNTO YOU

Date: July 8. 10:30 AM

The Seven Seals are the holy resonance bled into form by a porthole sort of effect through which all particulate matter travels in spirit form.

I was driving along in my white high top van on a hot summer day. Nothing out of the ordinary. Just on my way to drop off a few letters at the post office.

God took me up. In the middle of traffic. Without any consideration for my panic attack. I was suddenly hearing the creative mysteries from God and had no pencil in my hand nor paper to write down these mysteries.

Jesus! Oh Lord! I can see the whole picture! Wait! Lord, wait! Please wait for me to pull over to get some paper God!

In this porthole effect there is a wall surrounding the whole of your earth's dimension and diodeic holographic ...

Oh my God! I'm driving! How am I supposed to remember this?

Earth's Seal is bended by way of God allegro to your form in personified matter.

I maneuvered my vehicle into the right lane. Looked frantically for a place to quickly get out of traffic.
Slow down, God!

I tell you it is not I who slows down for you. It is you who is slowed down by me, your Creator. Spacial causations have your dimension interceded to blend fulcrum like to my Hand's desire.

What God?!
I pulled into the parking lot at a nearby fast food restaurant.

It is not I who slows down for you, Sharon. It is you who are slowed down, my dear, by the rotational pull into the holy dimensions that are you.

I screeched into an open parking space. Flung the contents of my purse hither skither out onto the passenger seat and found a pen. No paper. I grabbed my electric bill and wrote down God's words before I forgot them.
I had heard something quite amazing and I was becoming elated with expectation.
My spirit knew that this commentary would be a lengthy one.

Your spirit has Seven Strata to pass through. You, as man, are in Strata Three.

I'm in Strata Three?
I bought more time while grabbing my water bill to write on.
I knew from experience that if I did not write these Spirit words down I would never hear them again. They came once and only once. Never again would the exact phraseology come to me, the moment would have passed me by. I had to seize my Grace Window.

Strata three is the Third Dimensional voice placement to your formative self image. This means that the Third dimension of earth is where you form as Three dimensional, that is, as self which is Three dimensional.

In this porthole effect there is a wall surrounding holographic plane earth's diodeic value and this value translates diodeically through the grid fulcrumed Father's Way.

Whoa! In my wildest dreams I could not make up words like the ones which Holy Spirit told me this day.

Your earth's diode value is fortified, my children newly told my secrets, by me. I am Jesus and Father tells you His Way. These are the Seven Seals revelations, Sharon. I comment to you, Scribe, hear and write these things down, please.

Okay. God, can I go get my tablet of paper? It slid to the back of the van when I stopped! I was already climbing clumsily over passenger seats to retrieve a yellow lined tablet of many sheets of blank paper. I returned and sat in the driver's seat before God spoke again. He is such a gentleman. Waiting in the dilemma of a lady such as He did!

I say dear students of my school house, I am your Teacher, and this is the lesson Holy Unto You. Your walled in dimension of earth is fortified newly and refreshingly by me. Through this porthole entrance in effect the embrasure is the door or window into which you pass as you go to the next Seal. I reveal in my Love for you each, this next Seal includes the relatively sublime presence which you call Heaven's gated passage way.

In this place, Time ends as you know Time, and beginning is God's Holy Heavens. I call this Seal Four because it takes up a place in the equation of the whole and fixes the place in the graft through the Fourth dimensional pulling of you into this place, the Fourth Seal. It is Heaven, in your language, and more to this is there to tell. God is complexity and simplicity and All of these are lovely to know of. Kindly go to read first Corinthians two nine.

I grabbed my Bible which goes with me everywhere and found this scripture.

First Corinthians 2:9 *"No eye has seen, no ear has heard, no mind has conceived what God has prepared for those who love him."*

Reading the footnotes in the Bible helps me to understand what a scripture means. According to the footnotes, we can't imagine what God has in store for us in this life or in eternity. He will create a new heaven and a new earth (Isaiah 65:17); (Revelation 21:1) and we will live with him forever. Until then his Holy Spirit guides us. This world is not all there is.

Your spirit is your self. Your flesh, or human form, is your self image while in the Third dimension.
You have a voice placement because you, as spirit, are 'resonants', or 'resonance', which I record upon my universe as I will.
In the beginning was self as spirit. Over this was layered image. In the image of self were dimensions given. In the dimensions was life of the spirit matured. In the life maturity of the spirit was God's hand molding spirit. In the molding of spirit was all.
Playing sweetly upon the noted chart of which your essence is made you are my love, and so your song is recorded thusly.

Sharon, this word is for all my people, given to you in love. I shall refer to you as musical beings because you should convey to your minds the concept that you contain a verbal placement within the Seven Seals which is dependent upon your tone, or resonance, to my ears.

See a wall which is fortified from my perspective. It is opened. In the porthole effect the wall is opened from the inside to the outside by you, as mortal. This embrasure, or porthole effect, is the door or window into which you pass as you go into the next Seal.
These entrances are what I am calling the Seven Seals. Each a holy resonance bled into form by a porthole sort of effect. This means that these resonance bleed, or trickle through, slower than the rushing of the usual flow, or, are let into somewhere else from the main body.

What does that mean? I wrote down every word exactly as Spirit told me His Mind.

Bleed means that I permit you to enter. I let you. I release you from the confinement which was the previous Strata, or Stanza. Bleed means I admit you. And I allow you to be known in the expression of musical reverberato within the Seal of your admittance.

I let you into the Third Seal from the Second Sealed place, as in the letting of blood which drains out of the body. I am the Body. And I make known and reveal to you the percussion of this Stanza entrance before you have fully entered, so that as you come in, you have the percussion ability to chamber your tune to the fullness going on in this Sealed in dimensional spiritual existence location within the Holographic, Holographic, Holographic, yes I said the word holographic three times, place, this Stanza Resonance.

Did you say we open the door from the inside?

Placement of your voice impression opens the Seal. More on that later, Sharon. Kindly save yourself this heat and go into the fast food restaurant. I will still talk to you.

Heat in mid July in Texas in a closed up parked van is stifling especially when sitting on scorching hot asphalt. Sweat drops were rolling down my nose and landing on my pages of writing, but I had not wanted to move for fear that I would break this revelatory train of Spirit's communions to me.

Oh God, thank You! It is broiling out here! I am so glad that no matter how large a thing is going on in the universe of You, Lord, You still remember each of us individually are human beings. Thank You that You want us to be comfortable.

~~~~~~~~~~

PLEASE UNDERSTAND

Please understand that I am the body of the electrical source that you are created from.

In this procedure the power supply of myself 'lets', or gives you a power surge from myself, and you are 'let down' into the Seal of this surge's existence for awhile.

*I*n the Third Seal is the reverberation of human beings. My people are like unto shapes sounding like musical chords as they walk and talk the language of life and death in their journey in the Third Seal. From start to finish you are 'let' into each Seal by Holy Jehovah God and by the hand of My most Holy Sovereign will.

I sat in the booth of an ordinary fast food restaurant, after cleaning the grease and grime off the table top, after praying to God and saying to Him in true humbleness, "Thank You for what I am about to receive." I sat with my humble human notebook and wrote the Spirit's gifts and I understood His words. I knew He wanted me to just write them all down, and for that I was truly grateful.

In the letting of you, as in the letting blood out of my body, I am saying that I give to you the blood of My Self which is electrical longtitudinal patterns and sequences that take you towards the existence I am creating holy and beautiful for just you in my vast House.

If you are 'let down' then you are 'slowed down' and your power surge is diminished and altered to flow in a congruent yet translated pattern of sequences, slower than my Whole, yet able to sustain your entire human spirit this time within the Third Seal portion of God's plan. I subtract from my Source and make your power tabulations and then I give you life within this thing, and HOLY is the name of the thing I give into your really truly live place in spiritual existence within Holy Seven Dimensions, called Seven Sealed Dominions within HIGH, and Divided by Truth, into the Sealed portions. Always Truth, however, the Whole is not seen yet to your eyes in holy Three Stanza.

I love you each, **keep treating my Door to the other side as the place you keep knocking upon. I want you to ask for the treasures which are the places after the Door takes your tune and admits this tune into the Whole Picture of My Holy Mansions.**

I took a flimsy paper napkin out of the napkin holder and wiped my happy human eyes which were streaming with tears of joy. Untold Greatness was speaking to me and I could hear this Tune.

You have a created purpose in each Seal.
I would be very foolish to surge your voltage above the appliance of your self's capacity. I do not wish to fry you so I am very careful in my capacity calculations.

Fear not, Sharon. These are truly the words of your Lord Jehovah. Seeing me in abundance is very freeing.
In each step is the song of yours made most sweetly ready and sung to me as such.
Therefore if your resonance sounds not the chord which opens the porthole, then you do not pass into the next Seal.
If your resonance sounds to the embrasure to open it then wide swings the passage way for a brief birth moment in travel. And out of the previous you fall into the next stage. I let you into the next Seal's realm.
The Seventh Seal is God's realm in spiritual strata. Sharon, you see into the Word of the Lord Jehovah.

God, I know Your Voice. Just please tell me what is happening here? Amen.

Prepare to receive from me a revelation of my Mansion's secrets. I shall speak to you. And you shall be in knowledge by my Enlightenment coming from Holy Spirit. These wisdoms are to be freely given to others for freely are they given unto you. I plan to allow this to take place in my time and by my way. I need for you to wait. To wait to hear me release your words. Amen.

You just want me to write it down?

Sent to you my holy handwriting Scribe is the secret of my Seven Seals. The terms will be mortal ones to convey to you the passage through spiritual formation. Remember that you must experience each Seal. Each divisionary place is a dimension unlike the other dimensions. I seal off from the other dimensions the one you are presently in at any present moment that you are.
This is the revelation of the Seven Seals.
I am your God Jehovah saying unto my people, My Kingdom is made up of Seven Sealed in Godly dimensions. Seven Seals are in place within my Whole dimension and you may see them all if you follow me. Take the time to go to Galatians 6:7-8.

Yes, Lord. I'll just look that up right now.

Galatians 6:7-8 *"Do not be deceived: God cannot be mocked. A man reaps what he sows. The one who sows to please his sinful nature, from that nature will reap destruction; the one who sows to please the Spirit, from the Spirit will reap eternal life."*

I think I'm going to faint. Faint or go to sleep. I feel so tired and, Jesus, I feel faint and unable to go on. This is too immense for me to tabulate as truly happening to me. God, You are talking to me! I can hear You God! Please if I just pass right out on the table or fall out of the booth on the floor please help me, Lord.

I will explain these things to you over a period of many days and weeks and months. Go home and rest. The mission is that you hear my revelations and Seven Seals will be revealed to you, my Prophet and Scribe. Jesus Amen.

Very well. May I ask another question first?

Yes. Love, talk to me.

God, do You have seven sealed in places that we go to? I mean, are these seven places separate from earth? Is earth one of the places? Is earth the third place in the seven places?

Holy one, you see my countenance smile with joy to your heart. I can explain these things to you and I shall, but these days will be plenty, and will take much energy from your electrical reserve. I need to give you time. I give time into the earth to grow my crops. I shall grow this crop in you, Sharon.

Love, yes, there are three places to get to being a human being. Place one is the First Seal. I say that it entirely is in the farthest thermal place from your now condition as mankind.

I say that the Second Seal is entirely closed off from this place earth you are living in. God in heaven tells you that I make the places of your spiritual growth to my pleasure and to my advantage. I see you. I seed you. I water you.

In the earth, which, yes is the third of these places of Sealed dominions, sealed from the other, ...

Kindness says, how weary you grow. I cancel out the place of communion.

No, Lord, don't leave me. I can hear more, Father!

I have overloaded your tabulations. You are in shock now. I must translate this into your healthy condition and I do not give my people more than they can bear. Love, in the Third place, Sealed in as earth, my people are the reservoirs of my yardsticks of great measure. I am always measuring you, by notes, not of this earthly realm, notes from Heaven's Bank. I also give you threads of filaments to grow with, and this holy process is a day to day thing.

Jesus I am, and you know me intimately, Sharon. I take leave of you but the Seven Seals will be told to you. I am faithful to my Beloved. Amen, Christ the Whole Picture Amen.

~~~~~~~~~

Communions With Christ

I SAW MY PRIESTHOOD GIVEN UNTO ME

Date: October 28, 1996

On an ordinary morning, as I was typing at my computer and looking out my window at the red cardinals and vibrant blue-jays in our tall oak tree I was suddenly overcome with Jesus Divine Love.

The Holy Spirit of God spoke to me. Most surely within my spirit, as I find my way in Him, Love gave me a revelation so deep and within such a private holy place that I never, ever will forget receiving this revelation, nor will I forget the humble room I sat within, or the day, or the experience because it was so searing of my soul.

I heard the Holy Majesty of God say into me from within me:

"ROSE, SEE YOURSELF ON STREETS OF GOLD DELIVERING MY PEOPLE UNTO ME."

I felt God stop my life at this moment, so as to make me focus on Him. And I heard / felt / knew God's Voice call me to be a minister to His people. I felt / knew / heard God's Voice calling me to choose whether or not to take vows, at this moment, into His holy priesthood.

This was a very profound calling upon me. I saw a doorway. It appeared to me inside of my intellectual knowing, and also inside of my emotions which swooned and went quite away in a glorious sort of God given place ~ the place God provided to my spirit to be having this experience within.

It was different than my ongoing fashioning. This was a deeper revelation than the ones I had been receiving. I saw a very celestial choir singing beside the waters of my human condition which was being given a priesthood if I accepted it from our Lord Himself. I took communion there. I partook of the Divine Eucharistic State. I ate of the feast of Christ that He was giving to me in purest loving kindness to my wholly amazed condition.

I saw the Lord ask me questions, all of them I was asked in the ceremony of my accepting the holy priesthood that God had stopped my life to offer me, if I accepted this condition which had with it the ramifications of being quite a mystical priesthood, as well as a very physical human sort of calling, and with which I would walk out very human experiences of calling people into belief of Jesus, by my humble days that were going to be guided by Christ Himself, should I accept this offer.

This was a here and now GATE, the THRESHOLD, which we were at. I was standing at the GATE of the inner places that I had not been allowed to see before this, but which were simply the culmination of all the days of getting there by faith, and by the ultimate grace of God's mysterious ways.

And at this point God stopped my life and He let me know that from this point on out, if I was to accept His call, I would be traveling with Him into the chambers that were deeper than I had known to this point.

I was undone with the beauty of the offer. God has a way of telling me major things in my life at the most unexpected times and in the least expected situations. I know that I know that when I hear this Voice take me out of my hum-drum mediocrity that He wants to especially catch my attention to the magnitude of His words to me.

So I sat. Meticulously scrutinized by God and found to be worthy of a call into the priesthood. How are the ways of God so contrary to man's ways! I judge, He takes a vessel and transforms. He washes, I walk away from filth. Jesus comes and takes the sins of our life and with His resurrection Power makes us new and a fine white transparent thing that He can see right through, and with this, I submit, He is divine.

Even though I did not know what would happen, just the mere offer was so glorious that I began weeping with heavy sobs and many tears of immense gratitude for even being allowed to know there is such a THRESHOLD as this within Christ Jesus.
I would be taking the vows of a minister, and through Holy Spirit's will and by His divine and mystical providence to come to me in serendipitous splendor and in rapture most holy. And a priest, oh my LORD, a priest would appear after I walked through His door … I am a priest now.

Oh God of Glory! I would be committing my life to His holy service in all aspects and obligations and expectations of a minister of God. In full understanding of the total seriousness of this call I gave up trying to stop weeping, being totally overcome with the Holy Spirit's Love upon me, showering me with Gold from God, showering me with holy yearnings to serve and accept the call, showering me with baptismal joy. With greatest respect for the sacredness of the pledge I would be making if I accepted God's call I replied to God:

"I accept Your call upon me to minister. Please help me."

God replied to my vow:

"CARRY THE WORDS OF JOSHUA 1:6-9 WITH YOU THROUGHOUT THIS MINISTRY."

After our Lord and Messiah finished carving out within my spirit the place He took me to dwell with Him, I was allowed to return to my conscious state. I remember that I was taken within the diocese of priesthood and was shown the course of my life. All servant-hood. All pain. Much pain. And yet, even so being shown, I said yes.

When God had finished impressing in my spirit His Majesty within Jesus Christ, the Majesty that gave His only Son to die for our sins and to be all Love within us to wake up to ... when God had finished communing with me, which lasted quite a while in human time, I saw a Seal come forth and He stamped me with this Seal.

This Seal was heavenly, a making of which I was ignorant about.

I saw the Seal and knew the mystery of its meaning but was told that the meaning was mine to know and mine to reveal as His Holiness gave me utterances. And for this I simply said in the presence of God a very heartfelt and grateful "Amen!".

And after the Holy Spirit took me and imprinted me with the Seal, or the Christ, as His own, I was given even more gifts of a spiritual nature. And I say 'imprinted' to mean a Seal of all that was and, as Uncreated Glory, is to come, and, as now in time is totally my Savior.

I was then taken to a chamber where walls were glass ~ and all seeing was possible to me as I stood awestruck to be placed here In Joy and in rapture with God, my own dear Spouse. And when the glass walls were shown to me, I mean revealed to me as existing to know of, I was then released ... all too soon for my spirit's liking I may add ... for the place of glass was clear and I openly loved the view. But it was ended and I was then returned to my human consciousness and allowed, in this room of Sharon, to go to read my Bible.

I was allowed to go read my Bible. Oh what a mysterious thing I have just said! I was allowed to read the Word. He is the Word. I was reading the Spirit that is alive and breaths and walks and talks and IS Holy God! I was whisked into the mysteries and taken to 'see', by Spirit's own revealing Grace to me, Jesus Christ, the King on High and my Friend for Life. Amen.

Oh Joy, Oh Love. You are too good to me. And seriously I was so touched when I looked up the scriptures of Joshua 1:6-9 which are my instructions from God Himself as He anointed my Priesthood into His Priest~ship, the words I am to carry within my walk and within my heart and within my mind and within my love for others.

Joshua 1:6-9 *"Be strong and courageous, because you will lead these people to inherit the land I swore to their forefathers to give them. Be strong and very courageous. Be careful to obey all the law my servant Moses gave you; do not turn from it to the right or to the left, that you may be successful wherever you go. Do not let this Book of the Law depart from your mouth; meditate on it day and night, so that you may be careful to do everything written in it. Then you will be prosperous and successful. Have I not commanded you? Be strong and courageous. Do not be terrified; do not be discouraged, for the LORD your God will be with you wherever you go."*

~~~~~~~~~~

REASONABLE CONCLUSION

Oh how much
I would have missed
out upon
if I had not
said
'Yes' to God.

Every step of the Way.

Printed in the United States
130239LV00002B/2/P